Saline District Library

3 4604 91089 7007

W9-AMV-978

j792.8 Mac
Mack, Lorrie
Dance

WITHDRAWN

LONDON, NEW YORK,
MELBOURNE, MUNICH, and DELHI

Senior Editor Paula Regan
Project Art Editors Laura Roberts-Jensen, Amy Orsborne
Editors Ann Baggaley, Scarlett O'Hara
Designers Sunita Gahir, Poppy Joslin
US Editor Margaret Parrish

Production Editor Adam Stoneham
Production Controller Sophie Argyris

Managing Editor Esther Ripley
Managing Art Editor Karen Self
Publisher Laura Buller
Associate Publishing Director Liz Wheeler
Art Director Phil Ormerod
Publishing Director Jonathan Metcalf

Jacket Editor Manisha Majithia
Jacket Designer Silke Spingles
Jacket Design Development Manager Amanda Lunn

DK DELHI
Art Editor Nidhi Mehra
Assistant Art Editor Jomin Johny
Design Managers Sudakshina Basu, Arunesh Talapatra
Project Editor Antara Moitra
Editorial Manager Pakshalika Jayaprakash
DTP Designers Arvind Kumar, Sachin Singh,
and Bimlesh Tiwary
Production Manager Pankaj Sharma
DTP Manager Balwant Singh
Picture Researcher Sakshi Saluja

Consultants
Sheila Dickie, Dr. Andrée Grau,
Kate Prince, Dr. Rachelle Stretch

First American Edition, 2012
Published in the United States by
DK Publishing
375 Hudson Street
New York, New York 10014

12 13 14 15 16 10 9 8 7 6 5 4 3 2 1
001—181740—August/2012

Copyright © 2012 Dorling Kindersley Limited,
All rights reserved

Without limiting the rights under copyright reserved above, no part of this
publication may be reproduced, stored in or introduced into a retrieval
system, or transmitted, in any form, or by any means (electronic,
mechanical, photocopying, recording, or otherwise), without the prior
written permission of the above publisher of the book.

Published in Great Britain
by Dorling Kindersley Limited.

A catalog record for this book is available from the Library of Congress.

ISBN 978-0-7566-9797-6

DK books are available at special discounts when purchased in bulk for
sales promotions, premiums, fund-raising, or educational use. For details
contact: DK Publishing Special Markets, 375 Hudson Street, New York,
New York 10014 or SpecialSales@dk.com

Printed and bound by Leo Paper Products, China

Discover more at
www.dk.com

Dance

Lorrie Mack

SALINE DISTRICT LIBRARY
555 N. Maple Road
Saline, MI 48176

AUG -- 2012

Contents

◀ South Korean fan dance

◀ Competitive ballroom dancers

◀ The Mariinsky Ballet's *Swan Lake*

84 Barefoot and full of feeling

◀ Shen Wei Dance Arts'
"Re-III" from *Re-Triptych*

98 The magic of musicals

◀ *Singin' in the Rain* at
London's Palace Theatre

120 Breakin' and street

◀ Korean urban
dance troupe, Myosung

Dancing *around the world*

All over the world, people dance to celebrate special occasions or express their national identity. Dances such as the **Chinese dragon dance** and **Spanish flamenco** are famous across the globe.

Step back in time

People have danced their way through history. In every ancient culture that has left records in words or pictures—from Egypt and India to classical Greece and Rome—there is evidence that dance mattered. Through the ages, dance has been used to **express national identity**, and it still is today.

The sword dance was a mock fight

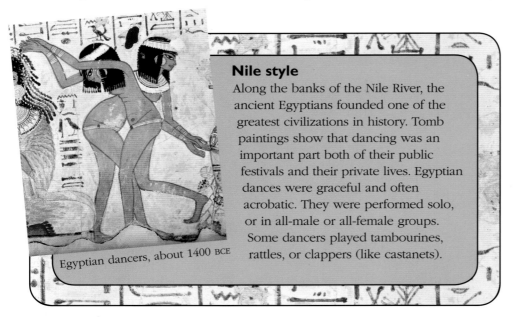

Nile style

Along the banks of the Nile River, the ancient Egyptians founded one of the greatest civilizations in history. Tomb paintings show that dancing was an important part both of their public festivals and their private lives. Egyptian dances were graceful and often acrobatic. They were performed solo, or in all-male or all-female groups. Some dancers played tambourines, rattles, or clappers (like castanets).

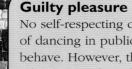
Egyptian dancers, about 1400 BCE

Greek for all

In ancient Greece, "dance" meant any body action, and included marching, mime, and even facial expression. Dance was thought to improve health and be part of a good education. The Greeks had a huge range of dances. Many were for ceremonial or religious occasions, or family gatherings such as weddings, while others were part of a wild night out. Performance dances had different names depending on the type of drama they appeared in—tragic or comic, for example. In Greek myths, the gods often danced, and dancing even had its own goddess, whose name was Terpsichore.

Guilty pleasure

No self-respecting citizen of ancient Rome would have dreamed of dancing in public. It was not considered the proper way to behave. However, the Romans accepted dance as part of religious rituals and were happy to watch dancing as a form of entertainment, either on the stage or in the street. They also enjoyed dance as part of a complex form of theater known as pantomime, which involved actors, singers, and musicians as well as dancers. As the Roman Empire expanded, travelers from its far corners brought a variety of new dance styles to pantomime.

Dance to honor Ceres, Roman goddess of agriculture

Old dances in the New World

For the native peoples of North America, dance is a major part of their lives. Over thousands of years, they have danced as a way of communicating with their gods, with each other, and with nature. Most dances are performed to the accompaniment of drums, which beat, so the dancers say, in time with the heart of Mother Earth. People often dance in a circle that represents the Circle of Life, which has no beginning and no end.

The buffalo dance celebrates good hunting

Dreamtime

There have been indigenous, or aboriginal, people in Australia for about 60,000 years—they are one of Earth's oldest civilizations. These people pass on stories about the creation of the world —called the "Dreamtime" or "The Dreaming"—through dances and songs. Some stories are performed by crowds of people, others by men or women only, but a few Dreamtime stories are told solely by people who have undergone special training and rituals.

Aboriginal dance at a festival in Australia

Pride of nations

Ireland has a surprisingly ancient dance tradition. When the Celts traveled there from Europe in 500 BCE, they brought dances with them. And when the Normans arrived in the 12th century, they added more dances. From these sources, the Irish developed a distinctive collection of folk dances. Irish dancing is now a popular entertainment, performed all over the world (see pages 12–13).

Dancing the Irish jig, 19th-century painting

Nataraja, the dancing form of Lord Shivadi

Inventing tradition

When the State of Israel was formed in 1947, national dances were specially created. These were intended to combine elements from older cultures with music and themes for the new country. Israeli folk dances are designed for everyone to enjoy. They are similar to line dancing (see pages 50–51), consisting of a simple, fixed sequence of steps that is frequently repeated.

Israeli folk dancers in Tel Aviv

Sacred steps

According to Hindu tradition, Brahma, the god of creation, decreed that because the scriptures were too difficult for ordinary people to understand, there should be a sacred entertainment to explain everything simply. This led to the creation of Bharatanatyam, a dance first performed in South Indian temples about 2,000 years ago by female dancers called devadasis. The style involves a straight back and bent knees turned out to the sides, with graceful hand gestures (*mudras*) that help tell the stories in the songs. Today, Bharatanatyam is widely learned and performed (see page 114).

Irish dancing

The Irish have been **dancing lively jigs and reels** since at least the 16th century. Modern Irish dancing is performed for fun at *ceilis* (dances) or competitively at *feisanna* (cultural festivals). The dancers perform solo or as a team. Irish music played on a piano, accordian, and bodhran drum is essential to the dance.

"Irish dancing is challenging—but really fun!"
Isadora

Overjump

Dancers begin with light-shoe styles, including reels and jigs. The overjump is a standard move in a light-shoe reel. The dancer needs to build up some height and momentum in order to perform the move well. She must look graceful and also stay light on her feet.

Starting position

Hopping

1

With a hop on the left foot, the dancer bends her right knee and tucks her foot up behind her.

Skipping

2

This is a travel step to build up momentum. Her right foot kicks forward, while she turns her feet out and points her toes. At the same time, she hops on her back foot.

Taking off

3

Now she is getting ready for the overjump. She pushes off from her left foot and tucks that leg up underneath her. Her right leg kicks forward, with the toe pointed.

▼ **Dance steps** There's a lot of very fast footwork in Irish dancing, including skips and high kicks when the body comes high off the ground.

Why is the upper body still?

Traditionally in Irish dancing the upper body stays still while the dancer leaps and kicks. The reason for this is to keep the top part of the body from distracting from the complex footwork that the dancer is performing. The gaze of the audience is drawn to the legs and feet to enjoy the skills of the dancer. Each dancer performs with a straight back and a pleasant smile, and looks proud. The goal is to make all that hard work seem effortless.

The foot is arched and the toes are pointed

Lifting up

4

Here is the most difficult part of the step—the dancer leaps up, raising her right leg to the horizontal and keeping it straight, while tucking her left leg back under her body. She keeps her upper body straight and strong, with her chin in and her arms straight.

Riverdance

In the 1990s, two shows exploded on to the Broadway dance scene—*Riverdance* and Michael Flatley's *Lord of the Dance*. Since then, Irish dance has become a worldwide phenomenon. There are now popular Irish dance schools all over the world, from Europe to the US, and from Australia to South Africa.

Dresses

In Irish dancing competitions girls wear dresses with long sleeves and a short skirt. Dress designs were originally taken from a beautifully illustrated medieval manuscript called *The Book of Kells*. Modern designs are simpler with bolder colors; some have hundreds of crystals sewn on to them.

Competition dress

Shoes

Irish dancing shoes are either hard or soft; hard shoes are for tap dancing and soft for light-shoe dancing. The tips of the hard shoes are made of fiberglass to give them their tapping sound. Some shoes have blocks at the end, like ballet shoes, to allow female dancers to go up on to the tips of their toes.

Hard shoes

Soft shoes

Hair and makeup

In competitions appearance is important and female dancers curl their hair or wear a curly wig. They also wear bright stage makeup and fake tans so that they don't look pale under the bright lights. Their poodle socks are glued on to the calves so that they don't fall down.

Wig and makeup

Twirling and stamping

These national dances all originate among people, native to parts of Europe and Asia, whose languages are classed as "Slavonic." Varying in style **from stately to boot-stamping**, they show how movement allows people to express their national differences, even if they speak languages with shared origins.

Simple style

The mazurka is a Polish folk dance that is thought to date back to the 16th century, or possibly earlier. By the 1800s, it had spread from Poland into the ballrooms of Europe. Simple and appealing, the mazurka involves mostly stepping, hopping, and gliding. This dance is often adapted for ballets. It can be seen, for example, in *Swan Lake* and *Coppélia*.

Dancing the Mazurka by Egisto Lancerotto

Polonaise partners

Noble march

A Polish national dance with a French name, the polonaise (which means "Polish" in French) developed from folk origins into a formal court dance in the 1600s. This aristocratic influence is seen in the dignified, promenading movements of the dancers. Polonaise couples link arms or hands and step gracefully around the room, occasionally turning under their partner's arm or bowing. The classical composer Chopin wrote the best-known polonaise music.

Dotty polka

The polka, a lively peasant dance, came from Bohemia (in the modern-day Czech Republic) in the 1830s. The name comes from the Czech *půlka* meaning "half-step." It was taken up in the ballrooms of Europe and North America when dancing was very popular—the newly fashionable polka dot pattern took its name from the dance.

Polka sheet-music cover

Strength and skill

The hopak (called *trepak* in Russia) developed from a men-only dance once performed by the Cossack warriors of Ukraine. Today, women also take part. The military origins of the hopak can be seen in some of the men's steps—acrobatic jumps, spins, and kicking squats danced with strength and aggression (right). The women sway and clap, and have spectacular turns of their own.

Men wear shirts with billowy sleeves and loose trousers tied with a sash

Young csárdás performers

Dancing in boots

The csárdás, the national dance of Hungary, appeared during the 1700s in the all-male atmosphere of country inns. Leather-booted men performed it with lots of stamping, heel-clicking, and boot-slapping. Later, the csárdás became a partner dance that starts slowly then gets faster and twirlier until it reaches an energetic finale.

Hopak dancer

15

Pattern *dances*

Throughout history, some of the simplest and most popular dances have involved groups of dancers moving in a special sequence to make patterns and shapes. The dancers form **circles, chains, parallel lines, or squares** by holding hands, linking arms, or placing their hands on each others' waists or shoulders. Pattern dances are always lots of fun to try.

Children dance in a circle in this 19th-century painting

Young girls dancing the hora

Around we go

One of the most common, and certainly the oldest, dance formation is the circle. In early societies, the circle may have symbolized togetherness or community strength, as everyone can see each other as they dance around. The ancient Albanian and Romanian version of the circle dance is the hora, which found its way into the Jewish community at the end of the 1800s. This dance is central to occasions such as weddings and coming-of-age ceremonies. It involves holding hands in a circle, stepping forward and back, and moving around to the right.

Folk group performing the quadrille on St. Croix Island, US Virgin Islands

Ballu tundu
performers

Living chains

Closely linked to both circle dances and line dances are chain dances. For the ballu tundu of Sardinia, Italy, couples hold hands tightly in facing lines. The formation is always moving, and the dancers are linked closely together, giving the effect of an unbreakable chain.

Get in line

"The longways dance" is another popular style of group dance that involves two parallel lines of couples who face each other to start, then step and weave around one another and other couples. Like most folk dances, these were originally country dances, fashionable in England and Scotland, in particular. In France, they were mixed with steps from French court dances and called contra dances (from "country dances"). It's in this form that they spread and grew popular in North America and around the world.

Illustration of a contra dance, 1810

Squaring up

Another well loved country-dance style is a quadrille, which is performed by couples in a square formation. Developed in 18th-century France as a court dance for Emperor Napoleon, quadrilles focused more on the patterns the dancers made than on intricate footwork or arm movements. Later renamed "square dancing," this became an important part of American culture—today it is the official dance in 19 states. Quadrilles were also taken to the West Indies by French and English settlers, and the African slaves adapted the dance to suit their own style. In Jamaica, a distinctive, local style of quadrille is part of the culture.

Mediterranean *moves*

For thousands of years, the people of the Mediterranean have seen their lands as the center of the world—the word Mediterranean comes from the Latin *medius* meaning middle and *terra* meaning land. It is a place where civilizations are **rich in culture**, and dancing is a vital part of national identity.

Sirtaki dancers

Simple steps with twists and knee bends

The dance of Zorba

It's hard to believe that sirtaki, one of the most famous and iconic of all Mediterranean folk dances, is not traditional at all. This dance was invented for a movie, *Zorba the Greek*, in 1964. Sirtaki is performed in a line or circle with dancers holding each other's hands or shoulders. Adapted from existing Greek dance styles, it starts slowly and gracefully, then builds to a fast pace with a strong, repeated rhythm. Today, some Greeks accept sirtaki as their national dance.

Jota performers

Spanish pride

Originating in the 1700s in northern Spain, the jota expresses fierce local pride. The name *jota* comes from a Latin word meaning "jump"—the dance is very lively and bouncy, with steps similar to those of the waltz. It is generally a partner dance. Like many folk dances, the jota has regional variations, and some people know where dancers come from just by watching the way they move.

▼ A statue in Barcelona, Spain, showing dancers performing the sardana.

Hands and feet

The sardana is a folk dance that comes from Catalonia, Spain. The dance is identified with the core Catalan values of harmony, brotherhood, and democracy. To perform this dance, people raise hands and move around in a circle using small, precise steps. The dancers follow a leader, who communicates through hand squeezes. At any time, more dancers can join in. When the circle gets too big, it divides to make smaller circles. Sardana music begins slowly, then picks up pace, getting faster and faster.

Tambourine

▲ Painting showing the tarantella dance, which is usually accompanied by tambourines.

Spider steps

An ancient courtship dance from Taranto, Italy, the tarantella was originally a quick and cheerful but graceful dance. However, a story goes that in the 1500s a strange ritual developed when people were bitten by the poisonous tarantula spider. They were advised to perform a frenzied version of the dance as a cure. Whether or not this is true, the dance has retained this energetic intensity.

Tarantula spider

In the beginning...

First appearance

The first recorded mention of flamenco was in a late 18th-century novel. It was danced mainly in gypsy homes and on the street. There was singing, dancing, and hand-clapping (*palmas*), but historians are unsure which instruments were used.

The golden age

The 1850s to 1910 was the era when flamenco turned professional. It flourished in *cafés cantantes*—venues where people paid to watch star dancers—accompanied by singing and guitar music. This was the birth of flamenco guitar.

John Singer Sargent captured the spirit of flamenco in his painting *El Jaleo* (1882)

Opera flamenca

Leading impresarios (people who organize concerts) took flamenco into big theaters and bullrings. They called it "opera flamenca" because opera was then taxed at a lower rate than other forms of theater. The dance became very popular, but purists believe it turned too commercial.

A formal dance

From the 1950s onward, flamenco began to be seen as an art form. Traditionally, dancers had learned by watching others, but now they began to have formal training. Today, many dancers study ballet or modern dance as well. Most people watch flamenco in professional concert or theater performances, or at a *juerga* (a spontaneous flamenco party).

La Quica, the great flamenco dancer, choreographer, and teacher, 1951

Fiery *flamenco*

A whole musical style that encompasses singing (cante) and guitar (toque) as well as dramatic dancing (baile), flamenco has its roots in the Moorish, Arab, Jewish, and gypsy cultures of Andalucía in southern Spain. Its popularity has **spread across the globe**, not only to the rest of Europe, but also to the Americas and Japan.

Face the music

The basis of flamenco is the music, which is classified by song styles or *palos*. Flamenco music is always sung, with guitars or other instruments. The styles all have different emotional moods, including upbeat festive songs that inspire dance (*alegrias* and *bulerias*), and more somber "deep" songs (*soleas* and *seguirillas*).

Paco Pena, one of the greatest of all flamenco guitarists and composers

Shell-shaped castanets are played in the palms to make a clicking sound

Take your pick

There are several flamenco styles: closest to its gypsy roots, flamenco puro is improvised and performed solo, with lots of hip movement. Classical flamenco is the style performed by modern flamenco companies—its signature features are an arched back, controlled hips, and extended, balletlike arms. Modern flamenco is very technical and involves intensive training, both in its fast, intricate footwork and its theatrical use of props such as castanets, shawls, and fans. Flamenco nuevo (new wave) has formal choreography and is influenced by other dance styles.

◀ Sara Baras dances in a sleek, unfussy style, with lots of foot stamping.

Dresses are long, ruffled, and usually made in bright colors.

Joaquín Cortés ▶ began his career as a member of the Spanish National Ballet.

Names to know

Here are some famous names to look for: Antonio Gades, whose movie appearances made flamenco globally popular; Sara Baras, who also stars in films and on television; Eva Yerbabuena, who studied flamenco from childhood and has won many awards; Antonio Canales, who trained in ballet before setting up a flamenco company; and Joaquín Cortés, who joined the Spanish National Ballet as a teenager and combines flamenco with ballet and modern dance.

All dressed up

Flamenco dresses are close fitting, with a flared, frilled skirt. A *bata de cola* is a dress or skirt with a long train. Dancers have low-heeled shoes with metal tacks on the toes and heels for loud stamping; fans; a *mantone*, which is an embroidered shawl; and flowers or combs in their hair.

Latin *mix*

Like many regions with strong dance traditions, Latin America is a **fertile mix of cultures** and races—there are the people who lived in these countries originally, the Europeans (mainly Spanish and Portuguese) who arrived in the 15th century, and the Africans taken there later as slaves.

Cumbia

Be my love

The cumbia was originally a courtship dance for slaves that developed in the late 1600s on the coast of Colombia. Couples gather in a circle and one couple at a time moves to the center to dance. Wearing or carrying a hat and bright scarves, the women swirl their long skirts and hold lighted candles to defend themselves against the advances of their partners. The cumbia is now the national dance of Colombia. It is one of the earliest Latin American dances, and the inspiration for a number of others including the salsa and the merengue.

Chilean courtship

The national dance in Chile is the cueca, one of many "handkerchief dances" found in Latin American countries. This courtship dance is based on a rooster and a hen—the male is aggressive, while the female is shy. Moving in a semicircle, the couple never touch but maintain contact with gestures and facial expressions. Both wave a handkerchief, which represents the rooster's comb or the hen's feathers.

The cueca is danced on September 18 each year

▼ The dancer who plays the deer wears a deer skin and a headdress made from the animal's head.

Preserving heritage

The Ballet Folklorico de Mexico was formed in 1952 to preserve and promote Mexico's traditional dances. There are two main companies. One is based in Mexico City, while the other tours across the world, performing national dances such as the *danza del venado* (deer dance) and "Revolution" (the gun dance).

The gun dance

Life cycle

The Mexican *danza del venado* (deer dance) is an indigenous dance, free of European and African influences. An ancient story-dance, it shows the life and death of a wild deer, a creature sacred to the Yaqui people of Sonora because it provided them with everything they needed. During the dance, the "deer" travels through the forest until hunters kill him for food, make shoes, clothes, and a shelter from his skin, and carve tools from his antlers, thus continuing the cycle of life.

Rattles around the legs create the sound of rustling leaves

Carnival fun

Bouncy and fun, the samba dates back to the 1500s, when the Portuguese landed in Brazil. The music and dancing of the African slaves they brought with them was combined with that of the native Brazilian peoples and the Portuguese to create a new and distinctive Latin American style of samba. As a solo dance, the samba soon became a defining part of the annual Carnival in Rio de Janeiro (see page 48). Further European influences gave rise to the samba style for couples that is now popular in ballroom dancing.

Samba dancer in costume

African *rhythms*

❝ *If you can talk, you can sing.*
If you can walk, you can dance. **❞**
Zimbabwean proverb

African dances are often based on a ritual or tradition. Some are dances of war, some of love, and some are rites of passage. In many cases, the dances are religious, **a way of communicating with gods** or spirits—to honor them, thank them, or ask for their help.

Congolese drum

Dance to the music

Across Africa, dance music is mainly produced by the drum and the human voice. Drums stir emotions and inspire feelings of belonging, while chanting crowds show their support. Dance is a group activity, and traditionally dances are done by both men and women, but not together in couples.

Trance dance

A ritual dance of Morocco's Tuareg people, the guedra is performed to create positive energy. Dancers drop to their knees and sway while making graceful arm movements and flicking hand gestures. The hypnotic drumbeat puts them into a kind of trance.

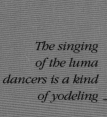

The singing of the luma dancers is a kind of yodeling

◀ The Baka tribe of the Central African Republic, Cameroon, and Gabon worship a guardian forest spirit and celebrate successful hunting with a ritual dance called the luma.

A guedra performance

Good hunting

Africans who depended on hunting for survival developed complex hunting rituals. The Zulus of South Africa have separate hunting dances for men and women. The men dance before the hunt, imitating the tracking and killing of prey. Zulu women dance in celebration, once the hunters return with their kill.

War dances

Today, many war dances are performed symbolically, rather than to celebrate battle. In the Zulu war dance called umghubha, spears and shields are held high. In Ghana, the Ewe people's agbekor dance imitates fighting tactics such as stabbing and surprise attacks. Performers also wave around horse-tail switches.

Les Ballets Africains troupe

Showcasing Africa

Formed during the 1950s in Guinea, the dance troupe Les Ballets Africains tours the world with its dramatic tribal dances, which feature leaping and shouting accompanied by djembe drums. In 1958, Guinea became an independent country, and Les Ballets Africains is its national dance company. It takes African dance to people who have never seen it, encouraging friendship with the rest of the world.

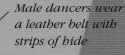

Djembe drum

Male dancers wear a leather belt with strips of hide

◀ This modern Zulu performer still wears the traditional costume.

Dancing boots

The gumboot dance grew up during the 20th century, in the gold mines of South Africa. The mines often flooded, so owners provided the miners with rubber footwear called gumboots. Forbidden to talk, the miners communicated by stamping their feet and slapping their boots. Soon, they refined this new language into a dance, which became a form of entertainment.

Gumboot dancer

Sticks, hoops, *and hats*

In many societies, traditional dances use specific props, either sticks to hold, or hats or bells to wear. The **props may symbolize ancient customs**, emphasize gestures, create rhythm, or express feelings. Sometimes, they simply enhance the movements of the dance.

Plate dances

In Asia, there is a long tradition of dancing with plates. The bhawai folk dance from Rajasthan, India, involves dancers balancing several earthenware pots on their heads. They do this while standing on plates placed on brass tumblers. The Uygur people of China also have a dance with plates and bowls. Dancers hold plates in outstretched arms, as they balance stacks of bowls on their heads, while raising one leg or skipping.

▲ A delicate balancing act, the bhawai dance is usually performed by women wearing colorful clothes.

Tall and strong

In some cultures, religious rituals involve dancing on stilts. In East and West Africa, the dancers on stilts represent gods or spirits. Wearing masks, they perform stunning movements to drumbeats. Africans in the West Indies perform this dance without masks, and for entertainment rather than religious reasons. In the Spanish town of Anguiano, stilt dancing is part of the local Catholic tradition, with dancers carrying a picture of St. Mary Magdalene.

Masked stilt dancer in Mali, West Africa

Ribbon dance

Round the maypole

In Europe, pole dances were originally a fertility ritual. The two main pole dances, the circle dance and the ribbon dance, are performed in spring (on May Day) or in summer. In both, people dance around a tall pole. In the ribbon version, dancers hold long ribbons attached to the top of the pole and dance so that the ribbons intertwine.

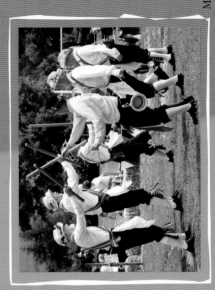

Morris dancers

With stick and sword

In English Morris dancing, groups of men perform rhythmic steps in set patterns, while touching sticks. Scottish sword dancing involves a solo performer dancing around swords laid on the ground. In "hilt-and-point" dances, common in Europe, performers hold swords that link them together in a chain.

Stilts are made of painted wood

Hoop dance

Circle of life

For most Native American peoples, ceremonial hoop dances (usually performed solo) show the "circle of life" from birth to death. A collection of hoops is placed around the dancer and, together with his body, form shapes that suggest specific animals, or features such as horns or wings.

Mexican sombrero

Hat tricks

The lively Mexican hat dance can be performed by a solo dancer, a couple, or a group. The basic steps involve rhythmic stamping, jumping, and clapping. The hat dance ends with a loud clap and a shout of *olé*—a Spanish victory cry. During the Mexican Revolution in the early 1900s, the dance symbolized national unity.

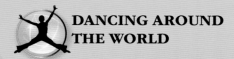

DANCING AROUND THE WORLD

Making the music

Percussive instruments are important accompaniments to dance as they keep the rhythm. Other reed or string instruments add the melody and can shape the mood of the dance.

Dhol

Bhangra is set to the fast beats of a double-sided drum called the dhol.

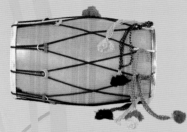

Zills

An Arabic dancer plays finger cymbals, called zills, as she moves.

Kathakali drums

The idakka, chenda, and madallam are wooden drums used in kathakali. Drummers hang them around their necks or shoulders and beat them with a stick to produce various tones.

Idakka

Surnai

Khattak is accompanied by a surnai—a type of wind instrument made of wood, with a bell at one end.

Beats from the East

In the traditional cultures of India and Pakistan, and the Arab countries of the Middle East, **dance has played an important role since ancient times**. These regions have a wide variety of dances, such as bhangra, kathakali, khattak, and Persian dance. Many of these dances are linked by their shared history and traditions.

Bhangra dancer

Bhangra pulse

A simple folk dance, bhangra was performed at the New Year and harvest festivals in the Punjab (a region of northwest India bordering Pakistan). With its lively steps, danced to singing and a pulsing drum, bhangra later became popular at weddings and general celebrations across India, taking on distinct regional styles. As Punjabis settled in other countries, they took the dance with them.

Khattak dancers

Sword play

Khattak was originally a warm-up exercise performed before battle by tribesmen in Pakistan and Afghanistan. The display of strength and spirit that once inspired warriors is still visible in the dance today. Wearing red vests, dancers spin and leap, each twirling two or three sharp swords.

Telling stories

Originating in India's southern state of Kerala, kathakali is one of eight Indian classical dances. Kathakali means "story-play," and performers use elaborate makeup, costumes, facial expressions, and hand gestures, as well as rhythmic steps and body movements, to tell stories. Originally, kathakali dramas were performed only by men. They were very long and based on traditional themes. Today, kathakali includes historical tales and stories from other cultures. Performances are shorter, and female dancers now take part.

Kathakali performers

Persian dance

Persian magic

Performed solo, Persian dance (Persia is the ancient name for Iran) puts emphasis on the upper body rather than the legs and feet. Dancers improvise, making circular hip movements and graceful hand gestures. Iranians often perform this solo Persian dance at family gatherings and private social occasions, where everyone sits in a circle around the dancer.

Arabian nights

Thought to be thousands of years old, Arabic dancing (also known as belly dancing) is popular the world over. Usually performed solo by a woman, the improvised dance includes rollings of the stomach and hips, combined with waving arms and shoulder and head movements. The dance moves vary in style from country to country.

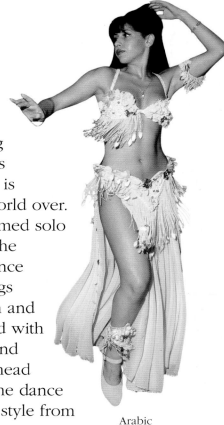

Arabic dancer

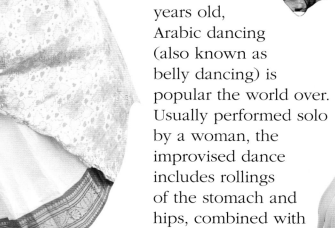

Dancers wear huge, flared skirts

29

Dragons, drums, and fans

For centuries, there have been close artistic links between China, Japan, and Korea, so their **dances share many cultural traditions**. In these countries, dancers typically stand firmly and move slowly in regular patterns.

Waist-drum dance

Dance for joy

The yangge was first danced about 200 years ago in farming villages in northern China, to give thanks to the god of the land. Today, it is a dance of joyous celebration following the New Year. An exciting element of yangge is waist-drum dancing, where performers beat a drum fastened to their waist with red silk.

Flowering of culture

The beautiful buchaechum, or fan dance, from Korea developed from ancient nature rites. The steps are graceful and controlled. The focus of the dance are the large, flower-painted fans of mulberry paper that the female performers carry. With astonishing skill, they use the fans to make patterns that represent waves, trees, or blossoms.

Fan dance

The power of the dragon

In Chinatowns across the world, the highlight of the New Year's celebration is a colorful parade led by a dazzling dragon. Considered sacred by the Chinese, the dragon winds its way through the streets in a dance intended to scare away evil spirits and bring good fortune. Skilled performers hold up the giant puppetlike dragon and leap, crouch, and turn to create the effect of a living, dancing creature.

Demon dance

In Japan, oni kenbai ("demon sword dance") has been performed for more than 1,000 years as a battle dance and to drive away evil spirits. Aggressive and masculine, the dance involves stomping on the ground and waving a sword as though preparing for attack. Performers dress as samurai (warriors) with breastplates and long-haired wigs.

Onikenbai dancers wearing *oni* (demon) masks, thought to bring good fortune.

Kabuki drama

Kabuki theater

Kabuki is a traditional form of Japanese dance-drama from the 17th century. Based on historical and moral themes, kabuki dances are performed on elaborate stages with dancers wearing colorful costumes. Originally women acted in kabukis, but later they were forbidden to take part. Even today, male dancers usually perform the female roles.

China National Ethnic Song and Dance Ensemble

In 1952, China's national performing company was formed, dedicated to the colorful traditions and arts of more than 50 different ethnic groups across China. Today, this company, together with the Light Music Orchestra of China, takes Chinese music and dance all across the world, acting as ambassadors of goodwill and friendship.

Dragon dance

Performers use poles to move the dragon's body

Strictly **ballroom**

From elegant waltzes to lively jives, ballroom dancing has something for everyone. TV dance competitions have **created a buzz** around ballroom, and dancers of all ages are now taking to the floor.

The story of ballroom

Shall we dance?

For hundreds of years, people of all ages have enjoyed dancing—often to celebrate special occasions or as part of a social scene, but also just for fun. Over time, the **wild folk dances of early centuries were tamed** into new dances suitable for elegant domestic rooms and public spaces. Social dancing, the forerunner of competitive ballroom, provided all kinds of people with pleasure, exercise, and the perfect way to make friends.

Medieval movement

We know that people danced during the medieval period (5th to 15th century) because dancing is mentioned in writings of that time, and shown in paintings and illustrated manuscripts. The dances survive in name only—for example, the ductia, trotto, and saltarello. One of the best known was the carol, or carola, in which the dancers joined hands in a circle while singing.

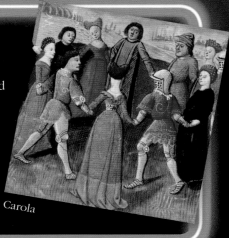
Carola

Flying feet

The clothes worn during the Renaissance period were not ideal for dancing. They were usually tightly fitted, heavy, and bulky to move around in, so dancers had to rely on their feet to produce most of the action. The steps were often lively and energetic, with much stamping, leaping, and turning. For the less nimble, two of the most popular dances were slow and stately—these were the pavane and the allemande.

Pavane

Renaissance line dancing

A few dance manuals have survived from the Renaissance (a period of cultural rebirth between the 14th and 17th centuries). These books give us some idea about the dances that were popular then. Most Renaissance dances were simple—couples usually performed them in lines or circles.

Minuet

French favorites

Between about 1600 and 1750, dancing was fashionable across Europe. The most popular social dances developed at the French court. One particular favorite was the minuet, a dance for two that involved moving with small, graceful steps. Another was the gavotte, a folk dance in which couples performed in a line or a circle.

Moving on

In the early 19th century, women's fashion changed from stiff corsets to soft, floaty dresses that allowed great freedom of movement. This made social dancing even more enjoyable, and it took place everywhere. People loved the polka, with its lively hops and steps, and the slower but more complicated schottische.

Polka

Mark my card

At formal dances (called balls) during the late 18th and 19th centuries, ladies carried a dance card, which hung from their finger, wrist, or waist. This listed all the planned dances by name or number. Gentlemen would book the dances in advance and enter their names on the card.

Cakewalk

International style

By the early 1900s, dance had become international. From the US came the strutting cakewalk and the lively jive (see page 49), and from the city slums of South America, the slow, sensuous tango traveled to the US, Europe, and beyond.

Scandal

Dancing reached a peak of popularity during the 1840s. By then, a new dance craze had swept across Europe—the waltz (see pages 38–39). For the first time, couples danced the way they do today—facing each other, with their bodies touching. This created a scandal that lasted for decades. Eventually, the polka adopted the same style, and it became socially acceptable.

The scandalous waltz took Europe by storm

New wave

In the 1920s and 30s, a wave of popular music such as jazz led to a burst of newly invented dances, many of which we still enjoy on social occasions today. From the 1940s to 60s, a standard set of rules was developed for competitive dances.

A wider audience

In the 21st century, television has created a new surge of interest in ballroom dancing. Live broadcasts of ballroom and Latin-style dance competitions—featuring celebrities and professional and amateur dancers—have gained a huge following all over the world.

Strictly Ballroom

Ballroom on screen

In 1992, Australian film director Baz Luhrmann produced Strictly Ballroom—a musical movie set in the world of ballroom competition. The movie was an instant international hit, mixing fabulous ballroom and Latin dancing with romance and gentle comedy.

TV's *Dancing with the Stars*

The world of **ballroom**

Social dancing has grown in popularity since the 1930s, and serious ballroom **competitions are now held worldwide**. Each dance has a detailed set of steps, and there are strict rules about the correct holds, posture, style, and dress.

The setup

Ballroom dancing competitions are held at two levels: professional (for those who earn a living teaching and competing) and amateur. The two main categories are "Ballroom" and "Latin." Ballroom dances include the waltz, Viennese waltz, foxtrot, quickstep, and tango. The Latin dances are the cha-cha-cha, rumba, paso doble, samba, and jive.

Junior ballroom competitors

Couples dancing the waltz at the Blackpool Dance Festival, a prestigious dance competition held in England

Dance your age

Amateur ballroom competitions are open to almost everybody. Sometimes there's just one category for dancers under 21, or there may be further divisions such as "juvenile" (under 12) and "junior" (12–16). In some countries, dancers are classified as "adults" when they are over 16, and "seniors" at the age of 35.

Judges awarding points on a television dance competition

And the winner is...

In competition, judges mark the dancers on different aspects of their dance, including posture, timing, the way they position their bodies as a couple, and how well they cover the dance floor. Couples perform each dance for between 90 seconds and two minutes, and are judged, alongside others, throughout the routine.

Formation style

All together now

Groups of couples can also compete in ballroom dances. There are two types of group dances: sequence and formation. In sequence, all the couples perform the same steps, in the same direction, at the same time. In formation, all couples do the same basic routine, but move in different directions to create a series of intricate lines and patterns.

Men's dress

In ballroom competitions men usually dress formally in tailcoats with a white bow tie and shirt. The tailcoats are most often black, although occasionally you may see gray or dark blue suits. Juvenile competitors don't wear tailcoats and instead wear black pants, a white shirt, and a black bow tie.

Man's tailcoat

Modern ballroom gown

Women's costume

Long ballroom dresses with full skirts and floats of material, to enhance the dancer's movement, are typical ballroom wear for women. Dress styles have changed over the years: in the 1950s dresses were much shorter with layers of netting; in the 1980s and 90s it was common to have ostrich feathers on the hem. Today, there is a huge variety in the color, styling, and patterning of ballroom dresses. Many are covered in rhinestones so that they sparkle under the lights on the dance floor. Women wear court shoes with a heel and suede soles. Juvenile competitors wear shorter, plain dresses, and their shoes have a block heel.

37

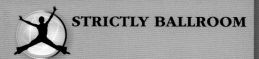
In the beginning...

Wicked waltzes

The word "waltz" comes from *waltzen*, German for glide or turn. Initially, the dance was declared "shocking" and "sinful." Not only did couples press their bodies together, but they could also do this even if they were complete strangers. The dance became popular internationally after 1816, when the British Prince Regent first allowed waltzes at society balls.

Dancing the waltz at a Viennese Ball

Waltz king

During the waltz craze of the 1830s and 40s, Austrian composer Johann Strauss II composed countless waltz tunes. He toured widely to perform them in vast new dance halls that could hold thousands of couples. Soon, Strauss's popular tunes earned him the title "the waltz king."

▲ Sheet-music cover of "Wiener Chronik" (Vienna Chronicle), a waltz performed by Johann Strauss II in St. Petersburg, Russia, in 1862.

Whirling waltzes

The graceful, gliding waltz is sometimes known as the "queen of dances." It is **a favorite on the performance floor**, danced in the classic style of the furiously twirling Viennese waltz or as the gentler version called the slow waltz. Many modern, more relaxed variations, such as the Cajun, the Mexican, and the Country and Western waltz, have also become popular.

Tales of Vienna

The first waltz craze involved a lively, whirling version that we know as the Viennese waltz. Originating in Vienna at the end of the 18th century, this dance developed from the early Austrian and Bavarian peasant dances such as the ländler. Although it appears to be a simple dance with limited steps, it is actually very fast and challenging. Couples travel counterclockwise, constantly turning one way, then the other. The Viennese waltz can be difficult for beginners because of the rotation and speed of the dance.

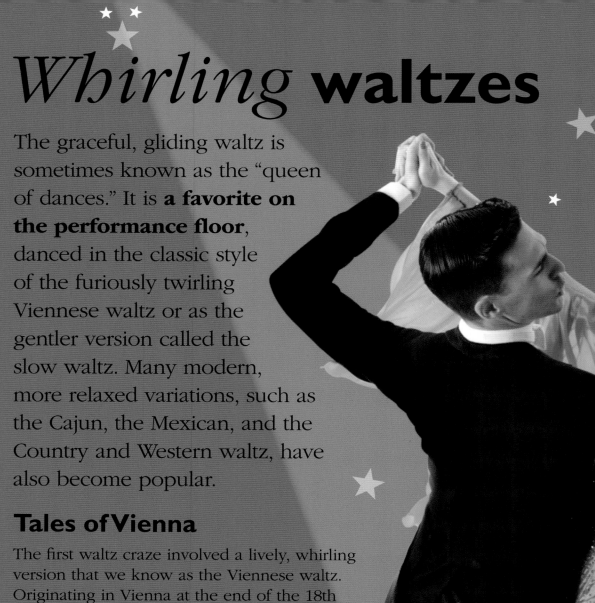

Men's tails are weighted to keep them hanging elegantly

Take it slow

Like the Viennese waltz from which it developed, the ballroom, or slow waltz turns, too, but gently and much more slowly. Couples move as one to the lilting music, and create beautiful lines (see pages 44–45). They glide around the room with extended, flowing movements that look almost effortless. The key elements of the dance—swing, sway, rise, and fall—are more pronounced in the slow waltz than they are in the faster Viennese version.

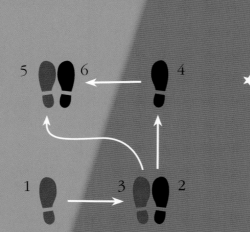

◀ During the waltz the man leads the steps and is in charge of the timing and the woman follows. The man's "forward progressive" step is shown here.

▲ Waltz music is expressive and romantic, and skilled ballroom dancers reflect this in their performance.

Wispy pieces of fabric called "floats" trail from a dancer's arms or wrists

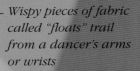

You shall go to the ball

The waltz is not just a competition dance, it's also a favorite at all kinds of social balls. In the famous story, Cinderella's first dance was a waltz and many modern "Cinderella balls"—usually fund-raising events for charity— also include waltzes. Costume balls often end with a waltz, and a newly married couple traditionally perform a waltz as the "first dance" at their wedding reception.

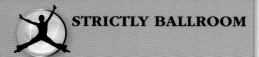
In the beginning...

Street dance

Most early ballroom dances were organized for the rich upper and middle classes, but the fiery tango came out of the poorest areas of Buenos Aires, Argentina. Toward the end of the 1800s, South America was settled by immigrants, many of them Spanish and African, who had brought their own dances and rhythms with them. Most were too poor for fancy gatherings, and there was no recorded music, so they danced the tango to bands in bars or on the sidewalk outside. Unlike the formal European dances, this exciting new street dance was improvised and its mood and style were distinctive.

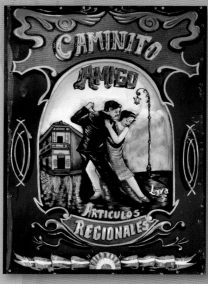

A street sign advertising the tango in the La Boca neighborhood of Buenos Aires.

Man to man

During the early days of tango there were more men than women in Buenos Aires. This mix of town laborers and gauchos (South American cowboys) had to work especially hard to attract a prospective partner, and one of the main ways they did this was to become graceful and polished dancers. Since there were not enough women to practice with, men had to perfect their skills by dancing with one another. Like other couples, they danced in bars or on the nearby streets when they had no money to spend inside.

Tango times two

There are **various ways of dancing the tango**, one of the most familiar being the style we know as "ballroom" or "modern" tango. Another popular version is the Argentine tango, which is freer and more flamboyant, and is danced to many different types of music.

Argentine tango show, Buenos Aires

◀ The ballroom tango, as shown in a French illustration from 1914

Ballroom tango

Originally, the tango was an improvised dance, but in the ballroom version the steps are performed in a fixed and formal style. Partners mostly keep contact at the hip, but arch away from one another with their upper bodies. In competition dancing, partners are not allowed to break their close hold. Ballroom tango involves frequent changes of direction. Dramatic body lines, together with short, crisp movements and stalking actions—often with sharp head flicks—create the excitement of this dance.

The man leads the woman from one step to the next

In a move called the sentada, the woman crosses her legs over the man's thigh

▲ Argentine tango dresses are typically knee-length with slit skirts. Men wear close-fitting shirts and pants.

Face the music

Tango music is as distinctive as the dance. It is usually instrumental, but is sometimes sung as well. Most experts agree that the tango has its origins in Spanish music but has also been strongly influenced by African rhythms.

Argentine tango

Since the 1980s, a form of tango that is seen more and more often on the dance floor is the Argentine tango. This improvised style is closer to the original tango than the ballroom version. Dancers move with bodies pressed together and legs crossing and intertwining. The Argentine tango is just one of many experiments with this 100-year-old dance. The *tango nuevo* or "new tango" is an ongoing development that began in the 1950s. It is the result of dancers loosening the movements and combining traditional tango music with jazz, classical, and other styles. The *neo-tango* is a more recent, extreme version that combines tango dance with techno and electronic music.

Tango shoe

American roots

Two highly popular dances in the ballroom world are the foxtrot and the quickstep. They **both had their beginnings in the United States** and are similar in style—although the foxtrot is subtle and elegant and the quickstep more showy and stylish. The foxtrot is one of several ballroom dances that can be performed the "American smooth" way.

"FULL OF ORIGINALITY"
THE "JELLY ROLL" BLUES
(FOX-TROT)

BY
FERD MORTON
AUTHOR OF "THE 'JELLY ROLL' BLUES" SONG

▲ Sheet music cover from 1915 for an early jazz foxtrot composed by Ferd Morton.

For men, formal bow ties and tails are customary

Glamorous and softly flowing, this dancer's dress is perfect for the graceful foxtrot

Foxtrot

In 1914 a music-hall entertainer named Harry Fox set the trotting steps he used in his routine to the newly fashionable ragtime music. "Fox's trot," as this was known, developed into the foxtrot. Eventually, the movements became much smoother, with simple walking and side steps, both slow and quick. The footwork of the dancers creates a gliding action as they move around the floor. A simpler version of the dance, known as the social foxtrot, is ideal for informal dances. In competition, it is an exciting dance to watch as couples travel elegantly around the floor in flowing movements.

In the modern foxtrot, steps are smooth, and gliding

Big-band beats

Quicksteps were originally danced to ragtime, a distinct African–American music style that was an early form of jazz. Soon, the quickstep and foxtrot were performed to jazz or swing-style music, made popular by the big bands of the late 1930s and 40s. Today, both dances are set to a wide range of musical styles.

British 1950s jazz band

Trombone

Quickstep couple

Quickstep

The quickstep with its springy style is much faster and lighter than the foxtrot. Influenced in part by the bouncy 1920s Charleston dance, quickstep dancers hop, leap, skip, kick, and run, with their feet hardly seeming to touch the floor. Quickstep couples need plenty of room to cover large areas of floor. The dance is stylish and playful; just learning the basic steps can be a lot of fun.

Smooth operators

American smooth is not a dance but a style. Since the 1920s it has been used as an alternative to the "European standard" style developed for ballroom dances such as the foxtrot, waltz, and tango. Smooth style allows dancers to open out from the closed hold position— which is not allowed under the standard rules. An "American smooth" foxtrot is livelier and jazzier than the conventional version, and dancers can break apart and do showy moves like solo spins.

◀ Famous dancers Fred Astaire and Ginger Rogers danced American smooth style in many of their movies of the 1930s and 40s.

43

Ballroom class

Every Ballroom or Latin dance has its own techniques and positions, which take **dedication and years of practice to perfect**. A skilled ballroom dancer makes these moves look effortless.

"School vacations mean more ballroom practice for us!"
Liam and Natalie

Elegant lines

Ballroom "lines" are the beautiful curved or straight shapes that dancers make with their bodies, by stretching from their toes to their fingertips. The oversway, throwaway oversway, contra check, and hinge are seen in swing dances such as the waltz and foxtrot, and some are also seen in the tango.

Throwaway oversway

The boy's right leg is stretched out behind his body, and his left leg is bent in front. He leans back away from the girl, and looks toward her. The girl mirrors the boy's position, creating a beautiful curve with her body and looking out toward the audience.

Oversway

The girl's shape extends to the left, and her weight is placed on the right foot. The boy bends his body to the right.

▼ Rumba routine

These basic steps in a rumba include "fan position," "alemana turn," and "hip twist."

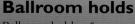

Baby ballroom

It can take time to become an expert ballroom dancer, and some like to get an early start. Children as young as three or four can enroll in classes and take part in youth competitions. It can be hard work traveling to classes and meeting up with dance partners, as well as competing at the weekend. For many young dancers though, ballroom is all about the fun and excitement of taking to the dance floor!

Young dancers celebrate their win at a juvenile competition

Ballroom holds

Ballroom holds—"promenade," "closed," and "tango"—refer to the correct positioning of the couple's hands and arms, and are an important part of the dance. In the promenade position, the couple form a "V" shape, with the boy's right hip touching the girl's left hip. Their hands are held together at shoulder level, and the girl turns her head to the right, while the boy looks left so that they face the same way.

Closed hold

This is the most common position used in most ballroom dances.

Hands held at eye level

Boy's right hand rests on girl's left shoulder blade

Girl rests her weight on her left foot, with her right foot pointing to the side

Tango hold

This hold is used only in the tango. It is similar to the closed hold, but is more compact, with the couple closer together.

Girl's left arm wraps around and underneath the boy's arm

Hands are slightly lower than in the closed hold

The couple stand with their feet close together, both with their left foot slightly forward and knees flexed

Contra check

Hinge

The couple stand with their feet in line and legs bent. The boy steps forward on his left foot, and the girl steps back on her right foot. Both keep their right heel lifted. The boy looks at the girl, while she leans back in an elegant curve to the left.

The boy positions his weight on his left foot, with his leg bent, and extends his right leg out behind him and slightly to the side. The girl also stands on her left leg, and stretches her right leg forward toward the boy's right foot.

Latin beats

The Latin dances are the **cha-cha-cha, rumba, samba, paso doble, and jive**. Unlike the ballroom dances, all five Latin dances have sections when couples can release their hold and dance apart from one another. Each dance has its own character and technique.

Latin dresses typically have much shorter skirts than ballroom dresses to show leg action

A dazzling Cuban-style rumba, performed by the Havana Rakatan dance company

Cha-cha-cha

With its origins in West Indian ritual dances, the cha-cha-cha gets its name from "cha-chas," a musical rattle filled with seed pods that was used by traditional voodoo bands. This dance first appeared in Cuba during the 1950s, inspired by both an earlier Cuban style called the mambo (see box right) and the American swing. It is danced to an easily recognized "cha-cha-cha" rhythm, and is characterized by straight legs and strong hip movements.

Cha-cha-cha competitors

Shoes have suede soles to allow dancers to move more easily across the floor

Latin costumes

Latin dresses are designed to be eye-catching and are usually short, sparkly, and colorful. Men wear close-fitting pants, usually in black, and their shirts are often covered in rhinestones. Dancers in beginners' competitions are restricted to wearing clothing without decorative embellishments.

Rumba

The rumba takes its name from the Spanish word *rumbear*, meaning to have a party or a good time. It's the slowest of the Latin dances and requires lots of strength and control from the dancers. Like many Latin styles, it has its roots in religious and ceremonial African dances, and involves accentuated hip movements. Because it is slow and sensuous, the rumba (sometimes called the "dance of passion") is particularly romantic. It often "tells a story," with the woman teasing her partner and then rejecting him.

The paso doble is characterized by curving body shapes

Paso doble

The paso doble (Spanish for "double step") is modeled on the traditional bullfights of Spain and Portugal. The man represents the matador (bullfighter), and his partner the cape. Dancers form dramatic shapes with their bodies and some of their steps are similar to those of Flamenco (see pages 20–21). The excitement of the dance is matched by the expressive music. Since the paso doble covers a lot of space, and is choreographed to highlights in the music, it is typically danced only in competition. It was once a dance for the ordinary Spanish people, but in the 1930s became popular among the fashionable upper classes in Paris. Some steps in the paso doble have French names—for example, *chassé* ("to chase").

Paso doble dancers

Roots and branches

There are many other Latin dances. Some of these inspired the official dances, and others have appeared more recently as variations of them.

Lambada

Originating in the 1980s, this Brazilian dance is defined by wavelike, side-to-side movements, and is danced on the balls of the feet, which are usually bare.

Mambo

This dance developed during the 1940s and inspired the slower, but more popular, cha-cha-cha. The mambo has roots in both the rumba and American jazz, and contributes the distinctive rhythm that is such an important feature of the cha-cha-cha.

Merengue

Older than many other Latin styles, the merengue is based in the folk traditions of the Dominican Republic. Light in feeling, the merengue has alternating fast and slow rhythms. Its signature move involves stepping out to one side with one foot.

Zumba

This Latin-inspired dance fitness style was developed in the mid-1990s, and is now danced in gyms and studios around the world. Zumba combines Latin and international music with high-energy aerobics and a mix of dance moves, including salsa, samba, mambo, and merengue.

Party *time*

The two Latin "party" dances that are part of competition dancing, the samba and the jive have a bouncy, exuberant, infectious quality. These **fast-paced dances** have their roots in Carnival celebrations (samba) and dance clubs (jive).

Samba

The samba has its origins in Brazil's mixed population—native peoples, Portuguese settlers, and African slaves. This dance reached the US in the 1920s. Samba travels around the room and the dance requires fast footwork, a samba bounce action, and an understanding of the different rhythms in the music.

Women's costumes have lots of sparkly decoration

Ballroom samba dancers

Carnival

The samba is danced at Rio de Janeiro's Carnival, a famous festival in Brazil in the days leading up to Lent (when Christians traditionally give up rich food and drink). The Carnival is a giant street party, with feasts, elaborate floats, costumes, masks, and music as well as dancing.

Jive

Of all the competitive ballroom dances, the jive is the fastest and most energetic. Although jivers do not move very far across the dance floor, the dance involves elaborate turns and kicks that emphasize the music's beat. Many movements are performed in perfect side-by-side unison. Lifts and jumps are sometimes seen in show performances or at social dances, but are not allowed in competition.

▲ When American soldiers came to Europe during World War II, they brought the jive with them. The dance developed out of lively, jazz-inspired American styles such as the jitterbug, swing, and the Lindy hop.

Social jive dancers often wear 1940s and 50s dress to reflect the dance's history

A jive lift

Salsa

Although it's not an official competition dance, salsa is hugely popular all over the world with both amateur and professional dancers. This exciting and romantic dance is a mix of Latin and Afro-Caribbean styles that came out of Cuba and Puerto Rico during the 1900s. *Salsa* means sauce in Spanish, and it came to refer to the hot and spicy flavor of the dance. A fast dance, the salsa has a strong side-to-side feel, with intricate swivels and turns in which the partners weave under each other's arms.

Salsa competitors

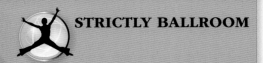

In the beginning...

Men only

Line dancing first appeared in North America during the 1800s, in all-male communities like mining towns. There were no female partners and this was a way for men to still enjoy music and dancing. Modern line dances were created in the late 1970s and have set, named sequences or routines that are repeated throughout a piece of music.

Billy Ray Cyrus

Music and dress

Early modern line dances used the music of the time, both rock and pop, and country. One lasting favorite is "Little Red Book," inspired by the 1976 Drifters single of that name. It wasn't until the early 1990s, however, when Billy Ray Cyrus released his huge Country and Western hit "Achy Breaky Heart," that line dancing acquired the cowboy-boots image that still endures. Today, it is danced to a huge range of musical styles, from pop to jazz.

Cowboy hat

Dancing for all

Ballroom and Latin-style dances are enjoyable and satisfying, but to progress and compete in these dances you have to learn and practice the strict techniques. Also, you usually need a dance partner. For **people who just want to get up and dance**, there are two fun alternatives that need no special training. They are line dancing and ceroc.

Get in line

Line-dance routines can be short or long, but the sequence of steps is always the same. Almost all have a built-in change of direction. In what is called a "two-wall" routine, dancers end up facing in the opposite direction from the one where they started. A "four-wall" dance makes a quarter turn to the right or left at the end of each sequence. All line dances are graded according to their difficulty, so beginners can start with short, simple routines and gradually progress.

Simple steps

Line dancers first learn their steps by walking slowly through the routine. It doesn't take very long to memorize the steps and start dancing.

 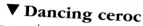

Ceroc around the clock

A version of the jive, called ceroc (from the French *c'est le roc*—"it's rock"), was created in the 1980s. This dance has basic steps, movements, and routines, which can be taught to large classes of students all learning at the same level. Dances can be slow or fast. They involve simple stepping in and out and turning, rather than the kicks and flicks of the competitive jive. There are lots of variations for more confident dancers.

Ceroc is like jive, but easier

▼ Dancing ceroc
In addition to classes, regular ceroc evenings are held in huge halls, where hundreds of people can enjoy dancing together.

In a ceroc class

Although ceroc routines are designed for dancing with a partner, classes welcome anyone who arrives alone. There are experienced and skilled professional dancers, called "taxi dancers," on hand to help beginners learn and to make sure that no one is left without a partner. During a class, dancers change partners all the time. Ceroc suits a wide variety of musical styles, from swing and rock and roll to modern pop. Dancers don't have to wear special clothes, just comfortable shoes with smooth soles that don't stick to the floor.

◄ Dancing in line
Everyone faces the same way and performs identical steps at the same time.

Classical **ballet**

Beautiful ballet is thrilling to watch and takes extraordinary dedication to learn. Classical ballets such as *Swan Lake* with their elegant *corps* of dancers, transport the audience to **magical worlds**.

The story of **ballet**

In the beginning...

Over several centuries, ballet developed from a simple court entertainment to amuse kings into a thrilling spectacle for everyone to enjoy. **Classical dance was perfected** in the great theaters of France, Italy, Scandinavia, and Russia, and now thrives in hundreds of countries around the world.

Ballet king

The seeds of classical ballet began to grow in the court of King Louis XIV, known as the Sun King, who loved dance and established a Royal Academy to promote it. It is because ballet developed in France that all the steps, positions, and instructions still have French names today.

Royal dance parties

In about 1450, during the Renaissance in Europe (a period of cultural revival), it was fashionable to organize huge pageants for royal occasions. These elaborate displays featured drama and music as well as formal dances performed by kings, princes, and courtiers. In Italy, where the Renaissance began, some of these early dances were called *balletti*.

Dancing at the Venetian court

Early stars

After the King's Academy was closed down during the French Revolution, the world's first ballet school was founded in 1713, attached to the Paris Opera, which in turn formed a company. By the early 19th century, it was presenting star dancers and choreographers such as Jules Perrot, who developed fairy-tale ballets in the Romantic style.

Pas de Quatre by Jules Perrot, 1845

Dancing in the north

Dancing had been popular at the Danish court since the 1500s. In 1771, an official ballet company and school were founded, called the Royal Danish Ballet. In its early days the company was led by dancer, teacher, and choreographer August Bournonville, an outstanding figure in ballet history. In 1773, King Gustav III founded the Royal Swedish Ballet in Stockholm, a respected company, although not as successful as its Danish neighbor.

Auguste Bournonville

Italian legends

During the early 19th century, the theater of La Scala in Milan was considered to be a leading center for Romantic ballet. One of the outstanding dancers of the age, Swedish-born Marie Taglioni, often performed there. Other famous dancers who trained at La Scala's excellent school included Carlotta Grisi and Pierina Legnani, who became a star in St. Petersburg, Russia.

Pierina Legnani

Imperial glory

It was in Russia in the late 19th and early 20th centuries that ballet really flourished. There were two outstanding ballet companies and schools: the Bolshoi Ballet in Moscow and the Imperial Ballet at the Mariinsky Theater in St. Petersburg. Here, sensational dancers, teachers, choreographers, and designers were all working to create the very best ballets that the world had even seen.

The Nutcracker at the Mariinsky Theater, 1892

Golden music

The golden era of Russian ballet began when ballet music started to be taken seriously. Until then, the music was mostly a patchwork of different pieces. But with Tchaikovsky's scores for three great 19th-century ballets—*Swan Lake*, *The Sleeping Beauty*, and *The Nutcracker*—the tide turned, leading to demand for quality music.

Michel Fokine, with Tamara Karsavina, in his 1910 ballet *The Firebird*

The new style

Big changes happened in ballet in the 1920s and '30s. Fairy tales, frothy white tutus, and magical stage sets were still popular, but modern dance styles (see pages 82–83) were developing. New-style choreographers and performers experimented with dance to tell real-life stories, or simply to express movement and feelings without any story at all. Their fresh outlook had a lasting effect on classical ballet.

Across the Atlantic

At the beginning of the 20th century, a new company, Sergei Diaghilev's Ballets Russes (see pages 56–57), took Europe by storm. Then two of Diaghilev's choreographer/dancers, George Balanchine and Michel Fokine, crossed the Atlantic. These pioneers carried the spirit of Diaghilev to the US, and ballet soon gained a American fan base.

Mikhail Baryshnikov

Escape to the West

It was mainly Russian ballet that enchanted everyone during the early 20th century. But soon, for political reasons, Russian dance companies—and ordinary Russian citizens—were prevented from traveling freely. The Bolshoi toured internationally for the first time in the 1950s, but security was strict. Then, in 1961, the young Rudolf Nureyev (see pages 78–79), on tour with the Kirov (now Mariinsky) Ballet, fled from the company in Paris. Over the next few years, other Russian dancers such as Mikhail Baryshnikov also escaped. Now there are no barriers and Russian dancers appear all over the world.

Ballet in movies

Since the 20th century, movies set in the world of ballet have been popular. Although most of these films show a backstage life that is far from real, they usually include plenty of good dancing. Lead roles are often taken by ballet stars of the stage. One of the first to do this was Moira Shearer, a dancer with Sadler's Wells Ballet in London, who starred in *The Red Shoes* in the 1940s. The great Russian dancer Mikhail Baryshnikov has also enjoyed success with movies such as *White Nights* and *The Turning Point*.

Moira Shearer in *The Red Shoes*

Broadcast live

Ballet has come a long way since it was an exclusive entertainment for royalty and rich aristocrats. In the 21st century, this wonderful dance form is reaching wider audiences than ever before. Many leading opera houses now broadcast live ballet performances to be shown on the big screen. Often, people can simply go to their local movie theater to enjoy watching world-class dance companies perform.

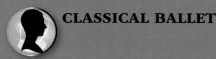

Biography

Sergei Diaghilev

1872: Born in Novgorod, Russia, the son of Pavel, a wealthy aristocrat and cavalry officer. His mother died when he was about three months old.

1896: Left university, where he had studied law and musical composition. As a student, he traveled widely and developed a love for the arts.

1899: Founded the journal *Mir Iskusstva* (The World of Art) with a group of artists and writers. Revolutionary in its time, the magazine featured essays on literature, art history, and criticism.

1900: Appointed as a manager with the Russian Imperial Theaters.

1907: Presented five concerts of Russian music in Paris and, the next year, a production of the opera *Boris Godunov*. As a result, in 1909 he was invited to organize a season of Russian opera and ballet, which was a huge success.

1911: Left Russia and established Diaghilev's Ballets Russes. For nearly two decades, the company toured many countries.

1929: Died, and was buried in Venice.

Influences

Richard Wagner (1813–1883)

As a young man, Diaghilev loved Wagner's music. After seeing a performance of one of his operas, Sergei wrote to his stepmother, "Everything is here… above all, it triumphs the truth of beauty."

Russia

Diaghilev was strongly rooted to the culture of his homeland. He never returned to Russia after 1911, but it was always Russians—painters, composers, and dancers—who dominated his productions.

Sergei **Diaghilev**

" *I have two idols—success and fame.* **"**

Although neither a choreographer nor a dancer, Sergei Diaghilev had a huge impact on ballet. He was an impresario, or organizer. The company he formed, called the **Ballets Russes**, made ballet popular across Europe and America.

Nijinsky in *Petrushka*, 1911

Signature style

Diaghilev-style ballets broke new ground, using startlingly free movements and blending dance with design and drama. The male dancers did not just show off the ballerinas—they had lead roles. Instead of one long ballet, Diaghilev often put on three or more short ones in an evening.

Winning scores

Before Diaghilev changed the world of dance early in the 20th century, a lot of ballet music was second rate—aside from the great works of Tchaikovsky. For Ballets Russes, Diaghilev commissioned the finest musical talents available (composers such as Igor Stravinsky, Maurice Ravel, Claude Debussy, Erik Satie, and Francis Poulenc) to write his scores. Sometimes, audiences were shocked or puzzled by the new sounds they heard. Diaghilev also used existing music, for example, Chopin waltzes for the ballet *Les Sylphides*.

Modern costume for *The Rite of Spring*

GRAMME OFFICIEL DES LETS RUSSES

Costume de "NARCISSE"

Russian artist Leon Bakst's cover for a Ballets Russes program

Designs on the century

Diaghilev was a source of inspiration to painters and designers. Two of his friends, Alexandre Benois and Leon Bakst, produced costume and set designs in intense, vibrant colors for the Ballet Russes. Later, well-known artists like Georges Braque, Pablo Picasso, and Henri Matisse were also involved. The Ballets Russes inspired fashion designers and was one of the main influences on the style known as Art Deco.

Mariinsky Ballet, *Les Noces*

Lasting legacy

When Diaghilev died, his company closed. Most of his dancers stayed in France and joined Les Ballets Russes de Monte Carlo, which lasted until 1952. Ex-Diaghilev dancer/choreographer Léonide Massine ran the similarly named Ballet Russe de Monte Carlo in New York. Diaghilev's ballets are still performed by major companies, and the creative people he nurtured have spread his influence around the world.

Dancing a story

The golden age of the **full-length ballets**, with their fantastic tales of love and tragedy, was at the end of the 19th century. Many of these big ballets still appear today, alongside extravagant new works created throughout the following century.

▼ **Giselle** Based on an old legend, *Giselle* is about a peasant girl who is betrayed by the man she loves. She dies of grief and becomes one of the terrible ghosts called Wilis, who lure men to their death. *Giselle* was first choreographed in 1841, but the version we know today was created in 1884 by Marius Petipa.

▶ **Swan Lake** The story involves a handsome prince, enchanted maidens, an evil magician, and the triumph of love. This is the most performed of all ballets, and the music, by Tchaikovsky, is familiar to many people. *Swan Lake* was a failure at its premiere in 1877, but became popular when revived later by Marius Petipa and Lev Ivanov.

▶ **Coppélia** This happy, playful ballet is about a toymaker named Dr. Coppélius who is obsessed with the idea of bringing a doll to life. His creation, Coppélia, is so lifelike that it fools the local villagers. When a young girl, Swanilda, sees her boyfriend Franz flirting with Coppélia she sets out to teach him a lesson. After lots of trickery and mistaken identity, all ends well. *Coppélia* is another ballet that owes its success to Marius Petipa, who in 1884 reworked the original version created in 1870.

◀ **Cinderella** The French fairy tale of Cinderella offers the perfect leading roles for a ballet—Cinderella, her prince, and the Fairy Godmother—and also makes good use of the *corps de ballet* as fairies, hours, and stars. Cinderella's two ugly stepsisters are character parts often danced by men. The version we know, with music by Sergei Prokofiev, was first performed in 1945.

Mariinsky Ballet principals Svetlana Zakharova and Igor Zelensky as the Swan Queen Odette and Prince Siegfried in *Swan Lake*

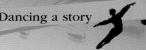

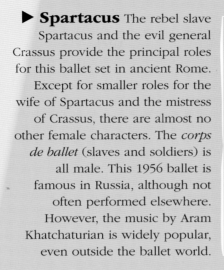

Spartacus The rebel slave Spartacus and the evil general Crassus provide the principal roles for this ballet set in ancient Rome. Except for smaller roles for the wife of Spartacus and the mistress of Crassus, there are almost no other female characters. The *corps de ballet* (slaves and soldiers) is all male. This 1956 ballet is famous in Russia, although not often performed elsewhere. However, the music by Aram Khatchaturian is widely popular, even outside the ballet world.

The Sleeping Beauty Princess Aurora is cursed at her baptism by an evil fairy. One day, so the curse goes, the princess will prick her finger on a needle and die. But the spell is altered by a good fairy, and when Aurora pricks her finger she simply falls into a deep sleep. No one can rouse her, until a handsome prince awakens her with a kiss a hundred years later. Music by Tchaikovsky and choreography by Petipa have made this ballet a firm favorite since its first staging in 1890.

Manon Based on an 18th-century French novel, *Manon* follows the fortunes of a girl torn between a longing for wealth and her love for a young student. The ballet ends tragically with Manon's death in the Louisiana swamps. Created by choreographer Kenneth MacMillan in 1974, *Manon* is popular with dance companies internationally.

La Fille mal gardée (The Wayward Daughter) This comic rural tale was first performed as a ballet in 1789. The heroine is a young girl, Lise, who thwarts her mother's attempts to marry her to a rich but unattractive farmer, and wins her real love, Colas. Frederick Ashton's modern version, choreographed in 1960, includes an exquisite pas de deux for the lovers, and a hilarious clog dance for Lise's mother (a role traditionally danced by a man). Farmyard animals and a tremendous rainstorm add to the fun.

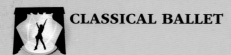
In the beginning...

A fairy tale

The Nutcracker was first performed at the Mariinsky Theater in St. Petersburg, Russia, in 1892. Marius Petipa wrote the libretto (storyline), which was based on a fairy tale called *The Nutcracker and the Mouse King* (1816). He was meant to choreograph the ballet, too, but he became sick so the dances were created by his assistant, Lev Ivanov. The piece wasn't a success and didn't become popular for another half a century.

Original costume sketch from 1892

What's the score?

To write the music (called the score) for *The Nutcracker*, the theater commissioned Pyotr Illyich Tchaikovsky, who had already written *Swan Lake* and *The Sleeping Beauty*. At first, the music was more popular than the ballet itself.

Tchaikovsky himself chose the eight pieces of music that make up *The Nutcracker* Suite

Pyotr Illyich Tchaikovsky

Hearing bells

For the celebrated Dance of the Sugar Plum Fairy, Tchaikovsky used an instrument that had only recently been invented—the celesta. Although it looks a bit like a small upright piano, the celesta produces a distinctive bell-like sound.

Celesta

The Nutcracker

Nutcracker doll

This magical Christmas treat is one of the most **frequently performed** of all ballets. People who have never even heard of it may recognize the music. *The Nutcracker* Suite, a selection of musical highlights from the ballet, was a huge hit in its day and is still highly popular.

The story goes...
The Stahlbaum's are having a Christmas party, and their little daughter Clara is given a special present. This is a nutcracker doll in the form of a soldier. During the night, Clara creeps downstairs to play with her new toy, but she is terrified by an army of ferocious mice. When she screams for help the nutcracker comes to life and attacks the Mouse King. Just when it looks as if the doll will be overpowered, Clara flings her slipper at the baddie and kills him. Suddenly, the nutcracker turns into a handsome prince. To reward Clara for saving him, he whisks her away on a magical sleigh ride. Traveling through the enchanting Land of Snow, Clara and her prince arrive at the Kingdom of Sweets, ruled by the Sugar Plum Fairy, who delights Clara by putting on a colorful display of dances. Later, the Sugar Plum Fairy dances with the Nutcracker Prince before he and Clara set off for home.

Different dances

In the Kingdom of Sweets, Clara is entertained with a fabulous array of dances—from Arabia, from China, from Russia, and from Spain. Even shepherdesses and garden flowers dance for her, and the music for these dances is some of the most familiar in the score.

Mark Morris's *The Hard Nut*

The Chinese Dance is part of Clara's entertainment

Another highlight—the exotic Arabian Dance

Cool takes

This widely loved ballet has been reinvented in lots of quirky modern ways. Choreographer David Bintley's *Nutcracker Sweeties* is danced to Duke Ellington's jazzy take on Tchaikovsky's music. In *Nutcracker!*, Matthew Bourne (see pages 94–95), has set the Christmas party in a bleak orphanage, while The Mark Morris Dance Group, dating the story to the 1960s and 70s, call their comic version *The Hard Nut*.

Change around

The story of *The Nutcracker* can vary slightly according to the company presenting it. Sometimes Clara (who can also be called Masha) is played by a little girl, and sometimes the role is taken by an adult ballerina, who later turns into the Sugar Plum Fairy. The midnight intruders are usually mice but can also be huge rats. In some versions, Clara wakes up in her own bed and realizes that her enchanted journey to the Kingdom of Sweets has all been a dream.

Matthew Bourne's *Nutcracker!*

David Bintley's *Nutcracker Sweeties*

Snowflake Dance performed by The Royal Ballet, London

Ballet *practice*

Training in classical ballet is the foundation of many dance styles, and most professional dancers started with ballet lessons at a young age. From prima ballerinas to Broadway dancers, the **daily discipline of practicing ballet positions** exercises all the body's muscle groups and produces flexibility, strength, grace, and precision.

"I love to try and make perfect positions."
Monique

Assemblé

Every ballet class begins at the *barre*—a handrail that supports dancers while they warm up. One of the first exercises is always a *plié* (knee bend). A *grand plié* is a deep bend, while a *demi plié* is a half bend. As with all ballet moves, *pliés* are done with legs and feet turned out from the hips, so the knees face to the sides. *Pliés* strengthen dancers' legs so they can jump. Here, the dancer is practicing a small jump called an *assemblé*.

Demi-plié
1

Swish
2

▼ Enchaînement

In a ballet class, after the students have warmed up, the teacher sets a sequence of steps called an *enchaînement* ("chain").

All jumps start with a *demi-plié*. Here, it is the back (left) foot that swishes out and the same foot that lands behind again after the jump.

The dancer swishes her left foot out to the side with it arched and pointed, and the leg is straight. To help with balance, the dancer uses her arms, making sure they form a graceful line.

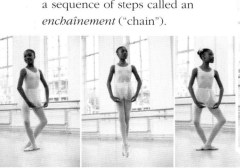

Legs are kept straight while jumping

Jump
3

Feet are pointed and held together

Land
4

As she jumps, the dancer brings her feet together and straightens both legs.

The dancer lands in another *demi-plié* to ensure a soft landing. The perfect *assemblé* sequence is performed in one quick, light movement.

Dressing for success

Clothes for ballet class should be comfortable, but they have to fit closely, too, so the teacher can see every position clearly. Girls usually wear stretch leotards and tights, while boys favor T-shirts and shorts or tights—both wear soft leather or fabric shoes. Hair should look neat and be held off the face and neck. Fingernails need to be kept short and jewelry removed, since it may scratch or distract the dancer.

Acting out

In traditional ballets such as *Swan Lake*, characters often "talk" to each other and tell parts of the story using a series of gestures, each with a specific meaning. These gestures have been used in ballet for many years. Nineteeth-century ballet audiences would have understood all the basic gestures, and ballet students still learn the same actions today. Common mimes include pointing to the engagement finger to show "marriage," or crossing hands over the heart for "love."

Love   Death

Training places

Today, there are ballet classes and schools in towns and cities all around the world. Most of the leading ballet companies run associated schools where they train their own dancers. Young children who attend these schools have ordinary school classes as well as ballet classes, while being trained to professional level. Some of the best-known schools run by ballet companies are the Vaganova Academy in St. Petersburg, Russia; the Royal Ballet in London, England; the School of American Ballet in New York City; and the Paris Opera in France. The world's biggest ballet school is the National School of Ballet in Havana, Cuba.

National School of Ballet, Cuba

Short **ballets**

A visit to the ballet often means watching one full-length piece with several acts. Sometimes, though, **companies stage a program** with two or three short ballets. Sergei Diaghilev's company Ballets Russes (see pages 56–57) almost always danced short pieces.

▶ **Lilac Garden** This exquisite piece was choreographed by Anthony Tudor to music by Ernest Chausson. A tale of tangled relationships, it is set during a country-house party in England in the early 1900s. Maude Lloyd and Hugh Laing (right) created the leading roles in 1936.

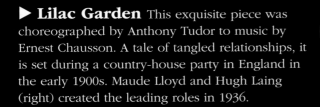

▲ **The Rite of Spring** For the Ballets Russes, Diaghilev commissioned Igor Stravinsky to compose a ballet about ancient rituals. This is Kenneth MacMillan's version.

▼ **La Bayadère** Some short ballets are chunks of older works that are rarely staged in full. One of the most extravagant is Act III of a 19th-century Russian piece, *La Bayadère*, featuring a ghostly *corps de ballet*.

◄ The Dream

One of Frederick Ashton's masterpieces, this work is based on William Shakespeare's *A Midsummer Night's Dream*. Set to music by Felix Mendelssohn, the ballet focuses on the fairy king and queen, Oberon and Titania (shown left, danced by Matthew Lawrence and Nao Sakuma).

◄ Pas de Deux

A varied program may include a spectacular *pas de deux*, from either a crowd-pleaser like *Swan Lake* or a lesser-known ballet like *Don Quixote*. Left, Paloma Herrera and David Hallberg dance *Tchaikovsky Pas de Deux*, a piece written for *Swan Lake* but never included in the full ballet.

► Fall River Legend

This ballet is based on a real 19th-century scandal in which small-town spinster Lizzie Borden was accused of killing her parents. The ballet was created by Agnes de Mille, who portrayed American life through dance in a series of memorable ballets and musicals (like *Oklahoma!*). The music is by Morton Gould. Here, Marie-Claude Pietragalla is Lizzie.

▲ Song of the Earth

This ballet was choreographed by Kenneth MacMillan to Gustav Mahler's songs about life and death. The songs were based on a collection of ancient Chinese poems, and the ballet sets them to movement. The leading figures are a man and a woman (Darcey Bussell and Gary Avis, above) plus a third character, called the "Eternal One" (Carlos Acosta).

▼ Jewels

One of George Balanchine's "plotless" ballets (see pages 68–69), *Jewels* has three parts: "Emeralds," "Rubies," and "Diamonds." Each features a different composer. Shown here is *Emeralds*, danced by Roberta Marquez and Valeri Kristov to Gabriel Fauré's music.

The choreographers

Choreographers are the controlling hands of ballet. They decide on the theme of a new work, choose the music, **invent or adapt the story, and weave the steps together**, sometimes inventing new ones. Then they choose and instruct the dancers who create the roles (dance them for the first time). The work of a great choreographer can be just as long-lasting as a piece of music or a book—each generation can enjoy it over and over again.

Leanne Cope and Kenta Kura perform the Puss in Boots dance from *The Sleeping Beauty*

▲ **Marius Petipa** In the history of ballet, no choreographer has been more influential than Marius Petipa. Born in France, he was Ballet Master at the Imperial Russian Theater in St. Petersburg at the end of the 1800s. Here, he created some of the big ballets now so well known, including *Swan Lake* and *The Sleeping Beauty,* and collaborated on *The Nutcracker* (see pages 60–61). He also reworked *Coppélia* and *Giselle* into the versions widely seen today.

Robert Helpmann and Margot Fonteyn in *Les Sylphides*, 1937

◀ **Michel Fokine** Russian-born Fokine studied ballet at the Imperial Theater School and graduated into its company in 1898. When Sergei Diaghilev (see pages 56–57) established his Ballets Russes, Fokine became the principal choreographer. He believed that capturing the true atmosphere of a ballet was more important than following the rules of classical dance. His *Les Sylphides* is pretty and romantic in style, while *Petrushka* and *The Firebird* are influenced by Russian folk tradition. After a century, all these ballets are still performed regularly by companies around the world.

▼ **Sir Frederick Ashton** Creator of the refined English ballet style, Frederick Ashton joined Ninette de Valois in London in the early 1930s, when she established her Vic-Wells Ballet, where he worked closely with Margot Fonteyn. In 1963, he became director of the company, by then The Royal Ballet. His ballets include *The Dream*, *La Fille mal gardée,* and *A Month in the Country*.

A Month in the Country

Antony Tudor teaching, 1942

◀ **Antony Tudor** Born in England in 1908, Antony Tudor later went to live in the US. He was inspired by ordinary people, rather than fairy-tale characters, and he was the first choreographer to explore human feelings through dance—Tudor could express sorrow or happiness with a simple gesture. Among his best-known ballets are *Lilac Garden* (see page 64) and *Dark Elegies.*

Song of the Earth

▲ Sir Kenneth MacMillan Like Sir Frederick Ashton before him (see opposite page), Scots-born Kenneth MacMillan was The Royal Ballet's resident choreographer and, later, its director. He respected the classical tradition while producing raw, powerful ballets, such as *Mayerling* and *Song of the Earth*. His version of *Romeo and Juliet* (see pages 76–77), is performed worldwide.

▶ Yuri Grigorovich
The leading Russian choreographer of the late 20th century, Yuri Grigorovich directed the Bolshoi Ballet for nearly 30 years, and created many of its major ballets. His best-known work is *Spartacus* (see page 59). Other important ballets are *Legend of Love*, *The Stone Flower*, and *Ivan the Terrible*. Grigorovich arranged over 30 tours to make the Bolshoi better known internationally.

Igor Yebra in the title role of *Ivan the Terrible*

▼ Christopher Wheeldon After training at the Royal Ballet School in London, Christopher Wheeldon danced with the company for two years before moving to New York City Ballet. He was appointed resident choreographer at NYC Ballet in 2001, and also produces work for other companies, including the Bolshoi Ballet. In 2010, Wheeldon created a new full-length ballet, *Alice's Adventures in Wonderland*, for both the National Ballet of Canada and The Royal Ballet (an arrangement known as a coproduction). The work uses stunning special effects as Alice grows and shrinks, and meets all the Wonderland characters.

Sarah Lamb in the title role of *Alice's Adventures in Wonderland*

Keeping track

Choreography was traditionally passed from one generation to the next through coaching by older dancers, but in the early 20th century, dance notation became widely used. Symbols representing positions are plotted onto a staff (set of five lines) like the one used for music. Two common systems are Labanotation and Benesh notation.

The jump of this dancer (right) in *La Fille mal gardée* is recorded in the Benesh notation shown below her. The feet are represented by the two marks in the middle of the staff.

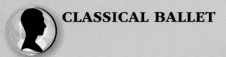
Biography

1904: Born Georgi Balanchivadze in St. Petersburg, Russia.

1913: Accepted into the ballet division of the Imperial Theater School, St. Petersburg.

1921: Joined the *corps de ballet* of the Mariinsky Theater (renamed the State Theater of Opera and Ballet after the Russian Revolution of 1917).

1923: Formed a troupe, the Young Ballet, to perform a new type of dance, which was disliked by the authorities of the new Soviet Union and soon abandoned.

1924: While on a European tour with a group of other dancers, he auditioned successfully for Diaghilev's Ballets Russes, where he worked as a dancer and choreographer until 1933.

1934: Arrived in New York City and established a ballet school there. He formed a small company called American Ballet, to dance at the Metropolitan Opera. This company broke up in 1938.

1946: After a long period working as a freelancer in the US and Europe, he returned to New York and, with Lincoln Kirstein, formed the Ballet Society (later New York City Ballet).

1983: Died in New York City.

New York City Ballet today

Influence of Stravinsky

Balanchine worked with the Russian composer Igor Stravinsky (1882–1971) for over 50 years; he organized three separate dance festivals dedicated to Stravinsky.

George Balanchine

❝ See the music, hear the dance. ❞

Choreographer and ballet master George Balanchine is best known for his plotless ballets—no story, no big stars or fancy costumes, just pure dance. He was inspired by music and **his dancers perfectly matched movement to sound**. Balanchine created over 400 ballets and founded New York City Ballet, one of the world's great dance companies.

Balanchine was a brilliant but demanding teacher

Prodigal Son, 1929

Diaghilev days

At the age of 21, Balanchine took on the job of choreographer for Sergei Diaghilev's Ballets Russes (see pages 56–57). He created 10 ballets for this company, including *Apollon Musagète* (*Apollo and the Muses*), with music by Igor Stravinsky, and *Prodigal Son*, to composer Sergei Prokofiev's score. Although these early ballets had a vague storyline, Balanchine's simpler dance style was soon to follow.

New York City Ballet dance Balanchine's *Serenade*

A new country

In 1933, a few years after Diaghilev's death, a wealthy American named Lincoln Kirstein invited Balanchine to the US. Together they established the School of American Ballet in New York City and its associated company, American Ballet. Balanchine staged several works at the Metropolitan Opera, but the venture was short-lived because they found Balanchine's style too daring, and he preferred to work without restrictions.

Slaughter on Tenth Avenue, a ballet created by Balanchine for the musical *On Your Toes*

New York City

Going solo, Balanchine took on a variety of work, including creating dances for Broadway musicals and Hollywood movies. In 1946, he and Kirstein formed the Ballet Society, later called New York City Ballet (NYCB). Balanchine stayed with NYCB and trained generations of distinctive dancers. He liked his ballerinas to be tall, long-legged, and athletic.

Music and movement

While many choreographers are inspired by stories or people, Balanchine started with the music. His knowledge of music allowed him to communicate in a unique way with composers such as Stravinsky (shown on the right in this photograph) and Prokofiev. Balanchine could produce a piano arrangement of an orchestral score, which proved useful at rehearsals.

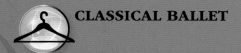
In the beginning...

Ballet slippers

A very popular dancer in the 1700s, Marie Camargo changed ballet dancing forever when she decided to dance in soft slippers rather than her usual low-heeled shoes. Her flat ballet shoes were tied on with ribbons, like modern pointe shoes, and allowed her to leap and land lightly.

Camargo in heels—before she began dancing in soft slippers

Costume changes

Ballet dresses, too, have changed over the years. In the 17th century, dresses had stiff corsets, which were difficult to move in. Marie Camargo had her dresses shortened so that her feet were visible, and also wore ballet tights (know as opera hose). Italian ballet dancer Marie Taglioni had a dress with a fitted bodice and a bell-like skirt when she danced in *La Sylphide*. This was a recognizable early ballet costume and dancers still wear it, in *Giselle*, for example. It's called a Taglioni or Romantic tutu.

A 17th-century ballet costume for a male dancer

Ballet **costumes**

Shiny satin shoes and a gorgeous frilly tutu are still the classic outfit worn by female ballet dancers. Ballet clothes **for practice and performance** have changed over the years, not only with fashion, but also with revolutionary fabrics and new techniques for making them. In addition to being beautiful, ballet wear also needs to allow the dancer to move freely and safely around the stage.

Embroidered tutu

▲ A new fabric

called Lycra (or Spandex) was invented in 1958 and had a big impact on ballet wear. It is flexible, lightweight, and strong, which means that dancers can move easily and freely. It is used for leotards (practice and performance), tights, and even the foundation layers of tutus.

Bright costumes for *Elite Syncopations*

◄ Performance costumes are

often made from Lycra because it doesn't restrict movement. Before the invention of Lycra, early fabrics were chosen for their fluid, floating qualities, so silk and muslin appeared often. Both then and now, costume designers also have to make sure clothes flatter the body and that they can be washed and worn many times without getting damaged.

▶ **In performances** dancers wear costumes that suit the historical period and the setting of the ballet. For example, the character of Swanilda in *Coppélia* wears a simple, embroidered dress to indicate that she's a peasant girl. Near curtain-up time, dressers go to each dressing room to help the dancers into their costumes and fasten the tiny hooks and eyes. Dressers also help with costume changes.

Costumes for *Coppélia*

Squirrel Nutkin in *Tales of Beatrix Potter*

▲ **Special costumes** can be amazingly elaborate and cover much of the dancer—including the head. These realistic animal costumes are a remarkable feat of design because, despite their size, they allow the dancer to leap and spin. They are designed to be lightweight and are carefully made to leave the legs and arms free to move. Complicated headdresses must have eyeholes that are large enough to allow the dancer to see the stage clearly.

Creating costumes

Before the costumes are made, the choreographer talks to the costume designer about the ballet and the historical period it is set in as well as the mood of the dance. Then the costume designer produces some ideas, sketched on paper, along with suggestions for colors and fabrics.

◀ **Modern tutus**, also called Classical, French, or "pancake" tutus, are short and jut out almost at right angles from the hips. These costumes are an astonishing feat of engineering, using multiple layers of net, graduated in size from inside out so the skirt forms the required flat, round, "pancake" shape. Often, a rigid hoop gives extra shape and support. Modern tutus are made from special nylon tutu net, which is incredibly strong with tiny holes, making it almost impossible to tear. The skirt is attached to a fabric basque (the flat part between the waist and hips). On top is a fitted bodice—this is usually boned to provide a smooth shape and support the dancer's body.

▶ **Ballet shoes**, usually made from soft leather, canvas, or satin, are attached to the foot with elastic. These are the kind of shoes that are worn by everyone for practice, and by male dancers for performances. When performing, female dancers usually wear special satin shoes with reinforced, or blocked, toes, and these are called pointe shoes. Before the dancer can wear her new pointe shoes she must sew on elastic and ribbon to hold them on. Many dancers also soften the block by hammering it onto a hard surface, and they put a layer of stitching or a sticky pad on the toe.

Soft shoes

Pointe shoes

Prima *ballerinas*

The word "ballerina" means much more than a female dancer. It's a rare and special title given only to the most gifted performers—the **stars of the ballet world**—from Anna Pavlova to Sylvie Guillem. Today, the term "principal" is used for the senior dancers in a company, although the most outstanding female dancers are still referred to as ballerinas.

◀ **Galina Ulanova** was a prima ballerina at the Kirov and Bolshoi Ballets, thrilling audiences in classical roles such as *Giselle* (left). She also earned fame in new ballets of the 1960s such as *Romeo and Juliet* (see pages 76–77).

▶ **Anna Pavlova** performed at the Mariinsky Ballet and Diaghilev's Ballets Russes. Later, she formed her own company, which toured in countries where ballet had never been seen before. Her signature role was Fokine's *Dying Swan* (right).

▶ **Margot Fonteyn** was an English ballerina who danced many principal roles when she was still in her teens. She joined the Vic-Wells Ballet (now The Royal Ballet) in 1934. The company toured widely, performing ballets such as *The Firebird* (right) and Fonteyn became the most famous ballerina of her time. In her forties, she established a partnership with Rudolf Nureyev (see pages 78–79).

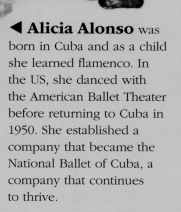

◀ **Alicia Alonso** was born in Cuba and as a child she learned flamenco. In the US, she danced with the American Ballet Theater before returning to Cuba in 1950. She established a company that became the National Ballet of Cuba, a company that continues to thrive.

◀ **Maria Tallchief** was the first Native-American ballerina. She performed with a later form of the Ballet Russes and created roles in several George Balanchine ballets. She married Balanchine in 1946 and joined him at the New York City Ballet. Tallchief's sister, Marjorie, was also a ballerina. She performed mainly in Europe.

◀ **Maya Plisetskaya** was a brilliant dance-actress and superb technician. She became prima ballerina at the Bolshoi Ballet in 1962. She was involved in creating many modern ballets, including *Anna Karenina*. One of her finest portrayals was of the title role in *Carmen* (left), with music from the opera and other Bizet pieces arranged by her husband, Rodion Shchedrin.

▶ **Lynn Seymour** was a great dramatic ballerina. Born in Canada, she studied at The Royal Ballet School and became a principal in 1959. She worked with Kenneth MacMillan (see page 67) and produced a stunning Juliet in *Romeo and Juliet*. For Frederick Ashton she created the role of Natalia Petrovna in *A Month in the Country* (right). In 1996, Seymour agreed to play the prince's mother in Matthew Bourne's revolutionary *Swan Lake*.

◀ **Marcia Haydée**, who was born in Brazil, was a ballerina at Sadler's Wells, London, where she was in the same class as Lynn Seymour and Antoinette Sibley. In the 1960s and 70s, she was at the Stuttgart Ballet, where she created many dramatic roles, including *The Taming of the Shrew* for director John Cranko, and *Song of the Earth* (left) for Kenneth MacMillan.

▶ **Dame Antoinette Sibley** was called "the perfect British ballerina." She joined The Royal Ballet in 1956. Early in her career she was partnered with Anthony Dowell, and they danced classical roles such as *Sleeping Beauty* (right). She also created modern roles such as Titania in Frederick Ashton's *The Dream* (see page 65).

The best of the best

In a ballet company there may be several principal female dancers, or ballerinas, and one or two prima ballerinas (*prima* is Italian for "first"). Very rarely, a higher title is awarded—prima ballerina assoluta. This is for the very few dancers who, in addition to achieving excellence in dance, have become well-known around the world—the title is really more of an honor than a rank.

More... *prima ballerinas*

The past century has produced some outstanding ballerinas, and in **each decade new ballet stars emerge**. Nearly all begin in the general group of dancers called the *corps de ballet*, talented dancers become soloists, and the most exceptional earn the title prima ballerina.

▶ **Cynthia Gregory** was declared "America's Prima Ballerina Assoluta" by Rudolf Nureyev. One of the best-known dancers in the United States for nearly 30 years, Gregory shone in roles such as *Giselle* and *Coppélia*. Here she is in rehearsal with Fernando Bujones.

◀ **Suzanne Farrell** was a tall, strong ballerina from the US. As a member of the New York City Ballet, she worked closely with George Balanchine and created roles in many of his works, including *Jewels* and *Vienna Waltzes* (left). She also made many guest appearances abroad.

▶ **Sylvie Guillem** was a frequent partner of Rudolf Nureyev when he was director of the Paris Opera Ballet toward the end of his career. In 1989, she left Paris to perform with The Royal Ballet for several years, and now moves between ballet and contemporary dance companies.

Sylvie Guillem as the Siren in George Balanchine's *The Prodigal Son*

▲ **Darcey Bussell**, at just 20 years old, became The Royal Ballet's youngest-ever principal. She shone in classics like *The Sleeping Beauty,* and in modern works like MacMillan's *Winter Dreams* (above), and became a role model for young ballet students.

▶ **Tamara Rojo**, raised in Spain, joined The Royal Ballet in 2000. She is a superb technician and an accomplished actress. Here she's the Queen of Hearts in *Alice's Adventures in Wonderland*.

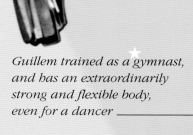

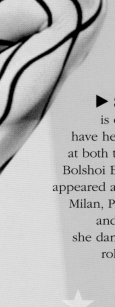

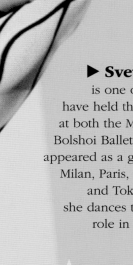

▶ **Svetlana Zakharova** is one of the few dancers to have held the rank of principal at both the Mariinsky and the Bolshoi Ballets. She has also appeared as a guest artist in Milan, Paris, New York, and Tokyo. Here she dances the title role in *Giselle*.

Guillem trained as a gymnast, and has an extraordinarily strong and flexible body, even for a dancer ⎯⎯⎯⎯

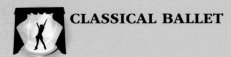
In the beginning...

First attempts

Over the years there have been many attempts to create a dance version of *Romeo and Juliet*, some as early as the eighteenth century. All of them fell flat—including a version put on by Sergei Diaghilev (see pages 56–57) for the famous Ballets Russes. It was not until the Kirov Theater staged its version in 1940 that *Romeo and Juliet* found its place in the ballet repertoire.

Galina Ulanova and Konstantin Sergeyev in the first production of Prokofiev's *Romeo and Juliet*

What's the score?

Sergei Prokofiev was commissioned to write the music for *Romeo and Juliet* by the Kirov Theater (now the Mariinsky) in Leningrad (St. Petersburg), and completed it in 1935. But the Kirov rejected the work as "too modern," so Prokofiev took his score to the Bolshoi Theater in Moscow—where it was declared "undanceable." Eventually, the Kirov went ahead with the ballet.

Take your pick

The first version of Prokofiev's ballet, choreographed by Leonid Lavrovsky, is still performed at the Mariinsky Theater. Outside Russia, many dancers and choreographers (including Frederick Ashton and Rudolph Nureyev) have created their own versions, but the most widely performed was the work of British choreographer Kenneth MacMillan for The Royal Ballet in 1965.

Royal Ballet dancers Lynn Seymour and Christopher Gable rehearse *Romeo and Juliet*, London, 1960s

Romeo *and* Juliet

William Shakespeare's tragic tale of teenage love has been retold endlessly. It has been used in **opera, film, and pop music**, and inspired the musical *West Side Story*. It is even a feature on Twitter called *Such Tweet Sorrow*. One of the most enduring versions of *Romeo and Juliet* is the 20th-century ballet with music by Russian composer Sergei Prokofiev.

The story goes... Renaissance Verona in Northern Italy is ruled by warring street gangs. Much of the trouble comes from the supporters of two families who have a long-running feud—the Montagues and the Capulets. Lord and Lady Capulet have arranged for their daughter Juliet to marry a wealthy nobleman, Count Paris, but when they give a ball to present her to society, young Romeo Montague and his friends sneak in wearing masks. Romeo and Juliet meet and fall in love, knowing that their parents will try to force them apart.

With the help of Juliet's nurse and a monk, Friar Lawrence, the lovers marry in secret. Everything goes tragically wrong when Juliet's cousin Tybalt kills Romeo's best friend, Mercutio, in a fight. Romeo kills Tybalt in revenge and is exiled from Verona. Friar Lawrence comes up with a desperate plan to help the couple escape together. He gives Juliet a powerful sleeping drug, which she takes to fake her death. Her grieving parents bury her in the family tomb. Romeo is supposed to be warned, so that he can secretly rescue Juliet when she wakes up in the tomb. But the message never arrives—all he learns is that Juliet has died. Griefstricken, Romeo breaks into the tomb to say goodbye and then kills himself by taking poison. When Juliet wakes and finds Romeo dead, she seizes his dagger and kills herself.

Dancing with death

The final heartbreaking scene of *Romeo and Juliet* is set in the Capulet family tomb. In Kenneth MacMillan's version of the ballet, this takes the form of an extraordinary *pas de deux*, which the grieving Romeo dances with Juliet's lifeless body. For the ballerina, pretending to be dead, but still looking graceful, is a big challenge.

Mariinsky dancers Evgenia Obraztsova and Igor Kolb in the final scene of *Romeo and Juliet*

Carlos Acosta and
Tamara Rojo as
Romeo and Juliet
with The Royal Ballet

Full of characters

In most stagings of *Romeo and Juliet*, only Juliet and her friends dance *en pointe*. Many of the leading roles don't involve much ballet because they are character parts, in which the performers do more acting than dancing. Juliet's nurse, for example, is an important character, and so is her mother, Lady Capulet. The part of Friar Lawrence, who marries the lovers and unknowingly contributes to their deaths, is also acted rather than danced.

In the Royal Ballet production, Friar Lawrence (Bennett Gartside) marries Romeo (Edward Watson) and Juliet (Lauren Cutherbertson)

Sword dance

Although *Romeo and Juliet* is a romantic story, it includes a lot of fighting. The Capulets and Montagues—and their friends and supporters—rarely miss the chance to take a swipe at each other with their swords. In a ballet, fight scenes like these have to be choreographed as carefully as any of the dances. The action must look realistic, but also balletic. Timing is crucial in a stage fight if injury is to be avoided. It can take hours of rehearsals to get a fight scene right.

Swords clash as Montagues and Capulets attack each other in a scene performed by the Mariinsky Ballet

Biography

1938: Born on a train crossing Siberia.

1955: Accepted into the school of the Kirov Ballet company. Three years later he joined the company.

Nureyev dancing as a young child

1961: Refused to return to Russia while on tour with the Kirov and asked France for protection.

1962: Made his first appearance with The Royal Ballet.

1977: Starred in the title role of the film *Valentino*.

1983: Appointed Director of the Paris Opera Ballet.

1987: Allowed to return to Russia to visit his dying mother.

1993: Died in Paris. His funeral was held in the Paris Garnier Opera House.

Other interests

Because ballet dancers have to start so young and train so hard, many of them never have time to pursue other interests. But even as a boy, Nureyev loved books, music, and paintings, and was particularly fascinated by the artist Vincent van Gogh. He continued to study and learn all his life, and could speak five languages.

Rudolf **Nureyev**

❝*Technique is what you fall back on when you run out of inspiration.*❞

One of the most famous and important male ballet dancers who ever lived, Rudolf Nureyev was also the first, and the only, **ballet pop star**. For a brief time, he made classical ballet cool in a way that it had never been before, and has never been since.

Nureyev as a student, partnering Alla Sizova in *Le Corsaire*, 1958

Born moving

Nureyev's mother was traveling on the trans-Siberian railroad to join her soldier husband when her son arrived earlier than expected. As a child, Nureyev loved folk dancing, but became inspired by a trip to the ballet. He was accepted into the state ballet school in Leningrad (St. Petersburg), and later joined the company. Although he started formal ballet training at the comparatively late age of 17, Nureyev was brilliant, although he was also difficult and fought against the rules.

Leaping free

Russian citizens were not allowed to move freely between countries, and the authorities suspected that Nureyev would try to run away if he went on tour. In 1961, a leading dancer was injured before a major European trip, and Nureyev went in his place. In Paris, about to fly home, Nureyev asked for police protection so he could stay in France. In Russia, he was convicted of treason in his absence, and cut off from his family.

Dancing the Blue Bird in *The Sleeping Beauty*, Paris, 1961

Birth of a star

Nureyev's dramatic escape from Russia made him an instant celebrity, and he never left the spotlight. One of his first performances was with The Royal Ballet in London, where he established a long career and a legendary partnership with Margot Fonteyn. Always restless, Nureyev also appeared with many of the world's finest ballet and modern dance companies, including that of Martha Graham (see pages 90–91). In his last years, he brought new life to the Paris Opera Ballet as its director.

With Margot Fonteyn in Frederick Ashton's *Marguerite and Armand*, 1963

Pop idol

Millions of people who know nothing about ballet have heard of Rudolf Nureyev. He set fashions with his quirky style, danced in discos with movie stars like Elizabeth Taylor, and starred in movies, including *Valentino*. He danced "Swine Lake" with Miss Piggy on *The Muppet Show*, and toured the United States in a revival of the musical *The King and I*. With all this, he still looked for new challenges.

Nureyev in *The Muppet Show*, 1978

One of Nureyev's most moving roles was as the tragic clown-puppet *Petrushka*

Setting the bar

Until Rudolf Nureyev came along, no male dancer had ever become such a star. Men were on stage largely to support and show off the ballerinas. Nureyev was a superb dancer—his solos were electric and he almost seemed to pause in the air when he jumped. He was also the first great dramatic *danseur* (male dancer). His heroes were full of fire and passion rather than being merely noble and elegant. Nureyev was the first major ballet star to cross over into modern dance. He largely inspired the free exchange between styles that is common today.

Dazzling *danseurs*

Today, **leading male performers** are known as principal dancers. Their traditional, and more romantic, French title was premier danseurs ("first dancers") and lesser-known performers were simply danseurs. Once, the role of the danseur was to support and show off his partner, but in modern performances men play a much bigger role and are as famous and adored as the ballerinas.

◀ **Vaslav Nijinsky** was one of the most famous dancers of all time. He was a brilliant technician and actor, as well as a gifted choreographer. After training at the Mariinsky Ballet, he traveled with Diaghilev and fellow Ballet Russes dancers to Paris, where he attracted huge audiences. Some of his performances caused quite a sensation—especially *L'aprés-midi d'un faune* (left).

◀ **Jacques d'Amboise** was a New York City Ballet principal who created roles in many Balanchine productions such as *Western Symphony* and *Stars and Stripes* (left). He also appeared in the Hollywood movies *Seven Brides for Seven Brothers* and *Carousel*. When he stopped performing he became a successful teacher and choreographer.

▲ **Robert Helpmann** was a great character performer and late in his career he was a memorable ugly sister in Ashton's *Cinderella*. He also had a featured role in the iconic ballet movie *The Red Shoes* (above). Helpmann was an early member of London's Vic-Wells Ballet (later The Royal Ballet). Born in Australia, he became a director of the Australian Ballet in 1965.

◀ **Vladimir Vasiliev** was a major star in the Bolshoi Ballet during the 1960s and 70s. Vasiliev conquered tough technical roles like choreographer Yuri Grigorovich's Spartacus and romantic heroes such as Albrecht in *Giselle*. His most frequent partner was his wife, ballerina Ekaterina Maximova—they sparkled in show-stopping *pas de deux* like this one from *Don Quixote*.

◀ **Patrick Dupond** is known for his flashy technique and dramatic style. They have made him a favorite with audiences, and also with modern choreographers, including Twyla Tharp, Roland Petit, and Maurice Béjart (see pages 82–83). During the early 1990s, he was director of the Paris Opera, where he trained.

▶ **Roberto Bolle** trained at La Scala, Milan, achieving principal status there before performing with many international companies, including the American Ballet Theater, The Royal Ballet, and the Tokyo Ballet. Bolle also makes special guest appearances at other events; here, he is performing at an 80th anniversary celebration for the fashion house Salvatore Farragamo.

▶ **Carlos Acosta** could have had a very different life if his father hadn't encouraged him into dance. As a teenager in Cuba, he started getting into trouble, but once he began ballet he was dancing leading roles before he was 20 years old. Based at The Royal Ballet in London, Acosta performs with other companies, including the Bolshoi Ballet. Today, he is the most famous male dancer in the world.

▲ **Ivan Vasiliev** joined the Bolshoi Ballet before he was 20 years old and a few years later he was promoted to principal. Stocky and powerful, he has an extraordinary jump, displayed to the full in roles like Spartacus (above). In 2011, he left the Bolshoi to join the more experimental Mikhailovsky Theater.

The modern touch

The pioneers of modern dance tended to reject everything about classical ballet. But there were many other dancers and choreographers who believed they could create **exciting new dance forms** that used some of the old traditions. Modern ballet was born nearly a century ago, but it is still full of surprises, and fresh forms continue to appear.

Roland Petit and his wife, Zizi Jeanmaire, in *Carmen*

◀ **Roland Petit** Born in 1924, Petit studied, and later danced, at the Paris Opera Ballet. He left there to establish the Ballets des Champs Elysées, the first of a number of dance troupes he led over the following decades. Petit worked on an astonishing range of projects, including Hollywood movies, and he created ballets for companies all around the world. Petit's wife, Zizi Jeanmaire, often danced in the works he produced.

Around the World in 80 Minutes, Béjart's final ballet

▼ **Robert Joffrey** Together with fellow dancer and choreographer Gerald Arpino, Robert Joffrey founded the Joffrey Ballet in 1956. The company offered an incredibly mixed repertoire, from *Billboards*, with a score by the pop star Prince, to revivals of old ballets such as *Petrushka*, first created by Michel Fokine (see page 66) over 100 years ago. Joffrey's company is no longer performing, but his experimental work has had a strong impact on 21st-century ballet.

▲ **Maurice Béjart** A contemporary of Petit (see above), Maurice Béjart formed several dance companies, the most important being Ballet of the 20th Century, based in Brussels. He was the first ballet choreographer to use electronic music, and he was fascinated by modern culture. In 1997, Béjart staged a work called *Ballet for Life*, based on the lives of Queen singer Freddy Mercury and dancer Jorge Donn, both of whom died young.

Valerie Robin and Fabrice Calmels in the Joffrey Ballet's *Light Rain*

▶ **Ballet Boyz** Former principal dancers with The Royal Ballet, Michael Nunn and William Trevitt created their own company, Ballet Boyz, in 2001. Their goal was to stage quirky work and also to give male ballet dancers an updated image. Ballet Boyz want to take dance to a wide audience, and their work is easy to enjoy.

William Trevitt and Michael Nunn in *Jianke*

Lynda Sing and Mathew Dibble in the Twyla Tharp Dance production *Known by Heart*

▲ **Twyla Tharp** As a young girl in California, Twyla Tharp had ballet lessons, and she studied tap, jazz, and modern dance, too. She also watched countless musicals, because her parents owned a movie theater. From the early 1970s, Tharp choreographed ballets that took in all these influences and more. For a while, she ran her own company, Twyla Tharp Dances. Today, she works in television, on stage, and for leading ballet companies. Among her best-known works is *Deuce Coupe*, set to music by the Beach Boys and said to be the first ballet to combine classical and modern styles.

The Mariinsky's production of *In the Middle, Somewhat Elevated*

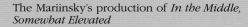

▼ **Pina Bausch** One of modern ballet's greatest innovators, Pina Bausch was Artistic Director of the Dance Theater in Wuppertal, Germany, which she founded in 1973. Her works combine dance with theater, and are often very dramatic. They include people talking, weird sets (such as a soil-covered stage), and strange music mixes.

The Brooklyn Academy of Music perform Pina Bausch's *Nefes*

▲ **William Forsythe** The creator of unusual and exciting 21st-century ballets, William Forsythe was born in the US, and trained there as a dancer, but first made his name in Europe. He worked as a choreographer with both the Stuttgart Ballet and then the Frankfurt Ballet and is now permanently based in Germany. In 2004, he established The Forsythe Company, which produces oddly titled ballets such as *In the Middle, Somewhat Elevated*, *You Made Me a Monster*, and *Yes, We Can't*. Today, William Forsythe's work is performed by many of the world's major ballet companies.

Barefoot and full of feeling

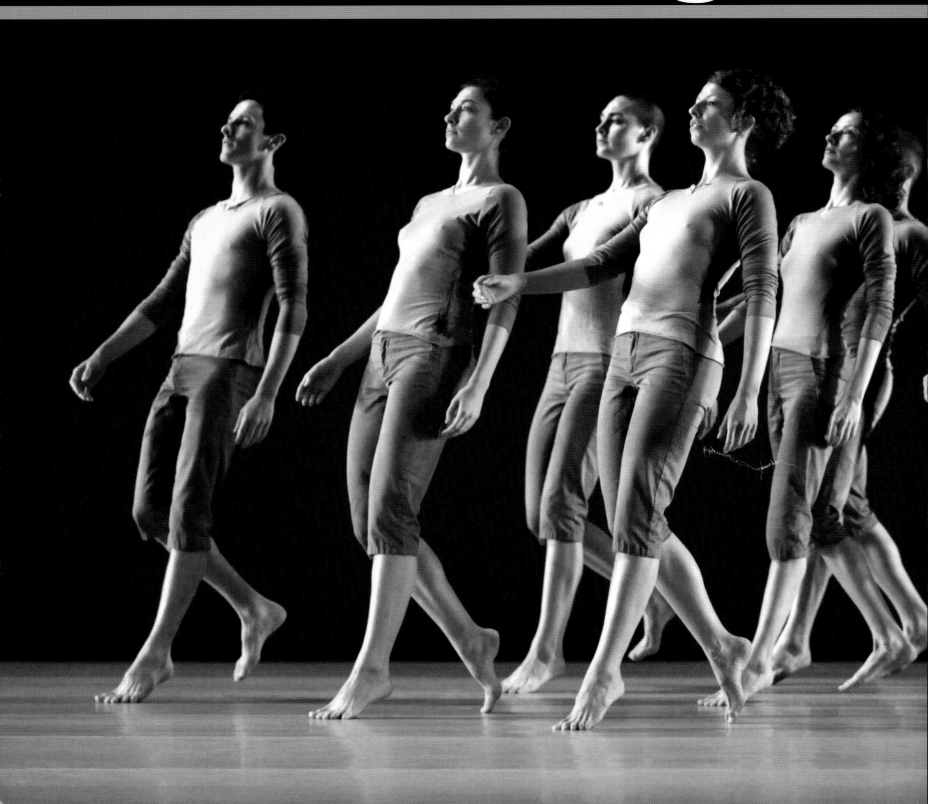

Modern dance started out as a rebellion against classical ballet and it was all about **expressing strong feelings** rather than telling a story. Now many dancers use both styles, or blend the two.

Pioneers of modern dance

Around the turn of the 20th century, some dancers and choreographers began to rebel against classical ballet. They thought it was too restricted and bound up in tradition and formal costumes. In the US and Europe in particular, many wanted to move freely and **express their feelings** and thoughts in whatever way they liked. These pioneers laid the foundations of modern dance.

Art Nouveau poster of Loïe Fuller in 1893

Artists' muse

Dancing amid flowing trails of silk and creating shapes with them using long sticks, Loïe Fuller choreographed her own performances. The way colored stage lights played on the silk was an important part of her work. Born in Illinois in 1862, Fuller started her career as an actress, singer, and stage-lighting designer. She turned to dancing later, in spite of having no formal training. Fuller danced mainly in Europe and was soon a favorite among artists; many painted or sculpted her.

Rudolf Laban with dancers of the Berlin State Opera in 1934

Master of movement

A pioneer of European modern dance, Rudolf Laban explored the theory and practice not only of dance, but also of movement in general (such as how workers move in factories). Born in 1879 in Hungary, he was also a great teacher, setting up schools in Germany and England. He invented a system of dance notation (recording movement on paper, like writing musical notes) that is still used—it's called Labanotation (see page 67).

Going with the flow

After taking a few ballet classes, Isadora Duncan decided that classical dance was rigid and unnatural and she was inspired to develop her own style. This flamboyant dancer was born in San Francisco, California, in 1877. She claimed to be inspired by the motion of waves and trees, and by ancient sculptures. Duncan danced with extravagant, flowing runs, skips, and jumps around the stage, always wearing filmy tunics and scarves. Introduced to audiences in Paris by Loïe Fuller, she performed all over Europe and Russia.

Isadora Duncan as she appeared on a 1904 magazine cover

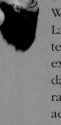

Mary Wigman performing *Dance of Sorrow*

Dramatic witch

Born in 1886 in Germany, Mary Wigman was a student of Rudolf Laban and carried forward his teachings. She focused on expressing emotion through dance, and her dramatic style rarely had any plot, or any accompanying music. One of Wigman's most famous solos was the *Witch Dance*, in which she performed distorted body shapes. Like her teacher, Laban, Wigman opened many dance schools in Germany and the United States.

Egyptian goddess

When Ruth St. Denis danced, she mixed wiggling hips, waving arms, and pouting facial expressions with gymnastic moves and popular dance steps. But she was very serious about her art. Like many pioneers of modern dance, Denis (born in New Jersey in 1879) began her career on the music-hall stage. In 1904, a cigarette advertisement featuring the Egyptian goddess Isis inspired her to create her own dance style. Denis was very popular in the United States and in Europe, where she toured extensively. With her partner, Ted Shawn, she established a dance school in Los Angeles (called the Denishawn School), and it was there that many influential modern dancers such as Doris Humphrey and Martha Graham (see pages 90–91) began their careers.

Ruth St. Denis performing in 1920

Doris Humphrey dancing with a large hoop in 1925

Free expression

Learning to love dance through an early career in ballroom, Doris Humphrey—born in Illinois in 1895—studied at the Denishawn School under Ruth St. Denis. Later she founded her own school with dancer Charles Weidman. For Humphrey, dance was not about spectacle, but about what the performer was thinking and feeling. She was interested in what she called the "fall and recovery" of the body, and used the weight of her body to show expression. Humphrey's work is still performed, and her book, *The Art of Making Dances*, is a valued resource.

Breaking barriers

Mexican–American dancer and choreographer José Limón (born in 1908) was a pioneer in breaking down the barriers between modern dance and conventional Broadway and ballet styles. Taught by Doris Humphrey, he performed with her company during the 1930s and also appeared in musicals. After serving as a soldier in World War II, he went on to found his own company, with Humphrey as Artistic Director. Limón created a range of dances, including *The Moor's Pavane*, a ballet based on Shakespeare's *Othello*.

José Limón (left) and Charles Weidman performing a twin leap

The modern way

While it's simple to define the principles of ballet (or tango, or tap), modern dance is more about what it isn't, than what it is. Pointe shoes are never worn—feet are either bare, or clad in soft, flexible shoes. Modern dance, like any other kind, requires training, but there are no set positions to follow, or specific steps to master. Dancers are encouraged to let their feelings mold their steps. Early purists had no wish to create a light, airy impression or hold an upright posture like ballet dancers do. Instead, body weight was used to emphasize movements, which were often performed on the floor.

Man behind the moves

Born in China, Shen Wei left home at the age of nine to study at opera school. He went on to become a founding member of Guangdong Modern Dance, the first contemporary dance company in China. In 1995, he moved to New York City, where he formed Shen Wei Dance Arts in 2000. Shen Wei also works with many other dance groups worldwide. In 2008 he was one of the lead choreographers for the amazing Beijing Olympics opening ceremony.

Opera with a difference

In China, the term "opera" refers to a form of traditional theater that combines music, acting, singing, mime, dancing, and acrobatics with elaborate stage design. In the past, these operas were based on history and folklore, but many modern examples are inspired by contemporary life.

The Beijing Opera Company in a modern version of a traditional tale: *The Legend of the White Snake*

The Shen Wei way

Like many modern choreographers, Shen Wei has created his own system of movement, which he calls "natural body development." He is concerned not just with steps and positions, but with "chi" (the flow of energy in the body), controlled breathing, and the way that bodies fit into the space around them. Shen also lets his dancers' natural instincts guide the way they perform his steps.

Shen Wei and his dancers in rehearsal

Shen Wei

One of the most imaginative forces in modern dance today is a company called Shen Wei Dance Arts, whose style **blends the traditions of East and West**. The fascinating—and sometimes mysterious—works produced by this group of dancers make use of art, music, and ways of thinking from both the past and present, and from many cultures.

Second Visit to the Empress

One of the classic Chinese operas that Shen Wei learned as a child was called *Second Visit to the Empress,* originally produced about 300 years ago. Shen has created his own version of this opera in a way that combines the ancient art forms of Beijing Opera with the unique style of his own contemporary dancers.

In *Second Visit to the Empress,* professionals from the Beijing Opera work on stage with Shen Wei's dancers

Connect Transfer

This work is sometimes called Shen's "paintbox piece." The dancers' bodies twine together to form swirly patterns that look like hand lettering. There are two versions of *Connect Transfer*. In both, dancers paint marks onto a canvas backcloth, transforming it into a piece of abstract art.

Rite of Spring

Like many other choreographers, Shen Wei was inspired by Igor Stravinsky's powerful music for the ballet *Rite of Spring*. The original ballet tells a dramatic story based on ancient religious rituals. Shen Wei's version has no plot—instead, his dancers move to reflect the patterns of the music.

Folding

Shen Wei is fascinated by things that can be folded—such as paper, fabric, and even people. In *Folding*, the dancers move slowly, bending their bodies to the sound of Buddhist chanting and to music by composer John Taverner. The performance shown above is in New York's Guggenheim Museum. It is a "site-specific" version of the work, meaning that the place in which it is held serves as an important part of the performance.

Designing for dance

At opera school, Shen Wei learned about theatrical art and design, and at one time he wanted to be a painter. He does his own designs for the costumes, makeup, and sets used in his productions. The illustration below shows a set design for Shen's work *Second Visit to the Empress*.

Biography

1894: Born near Pittsburgh, Pennsylvania.

1908: Moved with her family to California.

1916: Began studying at the Denishawn School, Los Angeles, where she later became a teacher, then a dancer with the company.

1923: Left Denishawn and moved to New York City to build a solo career.

1926: Formed the Martha Graham Dance Company.

1931: Created her choreographic masterpiece, *Primitive Mysteries*.

1969: Gave her last performance, in New York City at age 74.

1991: Died in New York City just before her 97th birthday.

The Company

Based in New York City, the Martha Graham Dance Company has a repertoire of over 180 dances. Her company has included famous dancers such as Alvin Ailey, Twyla Tharp, Paul Taylor, and Merce Cunningham, and her work has been performed by Margot Fonteyn, Rudolf Nureyev, Mikhail Bayshnikov, and Liza Minnelli, among others.

Influences

The body's voice

Martha Graham's father was a doctor who specialized in psychology—he thought he could work out how people felt by watching the way they moved. Dr. Graham always said, "Movement never lies," and this theory inspired his daughter's work.

Creative friends

Martha worked with composers Aaron Copland and Louis Horst, who created music for her work. Sculptor Isamu Noguchi produced scenery for her shows, and fashion designer Calvin Klein created costumes.

Martha Graham

" The body says what words cannot. "

For many people, Martha Graham is "the mother of modern dance." Born at the end of the 1800s, she **dominated the world of dance for decades**—both as a dancer and as a choreographer, and created a whole theory and language of movement that is still used today.

A dancer's life

Martha Graham started dancing when she was 22 (very late for a dancer) at the Denishawn School (see page 87) and stayed there for eight years before moving to New York City. She worked as a teacher, dancer, and choreographer before she formed the Martha Graham Dance Company in 1926.

Martha Graham and Robert Gorham in *Xochitl*, 1920

Members of the Martha Graham Dance Company during a dress rehearsal in Berlin, Germany

Martha Graham Dance Company performing *Appalachian Spring*

Stage effects

Having her own company allowed Graham to bring her ideas to life. One of her most famous works, *Primitive Mysteries* (1931), deals with religion and ritual. At that time nobody made dances about serious themes like these. Her fascination with American history led her to produce *Frontier* (1935) and *Appalachian Spring* (1944), celebrations of the American pioneers of the 19th century.

Modern movement

Martha Graham developed a special way of dancing, which used some unusual techniques. Two of these techniques were the "contraction" and the "release." They involve tightening and releasing the abdominal muscles while using carefully controlled breathing, and are still the basis of modern American dance. Graham's work features sharp, jagged shapes, instead of gentle, rounded lines, and sudden, jerky movements, rather than smooth, sleek ones.

Teaching methods

Martha Graham used special techniques to train her dancers. Classes began on the floor with the contraction, the release, and the spiral, which was a twisting of the torso around the spine. The dancers warmed up their feet and legs and began moving across the floor. Then they could start to put all the movements together.

Martha Graham teaching a dance class, 1954

companies

Modern dance doesn't rely on crowds of performers, elaborate sets, or traditional stories, making it easier for small companies to produce **exciting new work**. Today, contemporary troupes worldwide are attracting audiences with a form of dance theater that reflects their culture as well as experience of life in the 21st century.

▶ Merce Cunningham Dance Company One of the first to set dance to electronic music, Cunningham founded his company in 1953. He often worked with artists like John Cage and Andy Warhol, who designed the nature-inspired work *Rain Forest*, shown here.

▲ Paul Taylor Dance Company In *Esplanade* (above), Paul Taylor uses ordinary walking, running, and jumping moves to create a scene of pedestrians going on their way. The work is characteristic of this innovative modern dancer–choreographer. Taylor, who trained as a swimmer before studying dance, established his company in 1954.

◀ Alvin Ailey American Dance Theater The company's repertoire draws on music ranging from blues and gospel to the hip-hop interpreted in choreographer Rennie Harris's *Home* (left). Ailey founded his company in 1958 to promote African–American dance.

▶ Nederlands Dans Theater This company was set up in 1959 by performers from the Dutch National Ballet who wanted to be more experimental. In *Bella Figura* (right), choreographer Jirí Kilián puts together an artistic patchwork of different styles in dance, music, and costume.

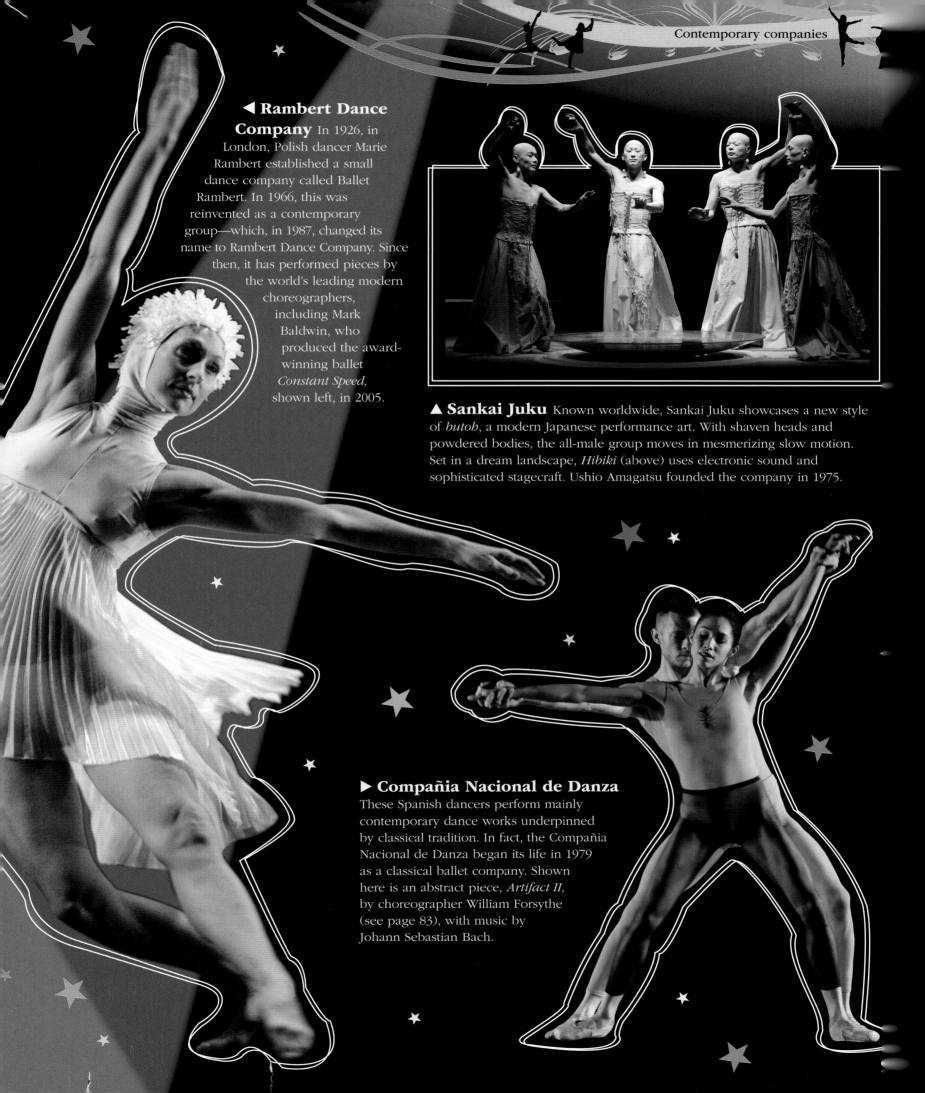

◄ **Rambert Dance Company** In 1926, in London, Polish dancer Marie Rambert established a small dance company called Ballet Rambert. In 1966, this was reinvented as a contemporary group—which, in 1987, changed its name to Rambert Dance Company. Since then, it has performed pieces by the world's leading modern choreographers, including Mark Baldwin, who produced the award-winning ballet *Constant Speed,* shown left, in 2005.

▲ **Sankai Juku** Known worldwide, Sankai Juku showcases a new style of *butoh*, a modern Japanese performance art. With shaven heads and powdered bodies, the all-male group moves in mesmerizing slow motion. Set in a dream landscape, *Hibiki* (above) uses electronic sound and sophisticated stagecraft. Ushio Amagatsu founded the company in 1975.

▶ **Compañia Nacional de Danza** These Spanish dancers perform mainly contemporary dance works underpinned by classical tradition. In fact, the Compañia Nacional de Danza began its life in 1979 as a classical ballet company. Shown here is an abstract piece, *Artifact II*, by choreographer William Forsythe (see page 83), with music by Johann Sebastian Bach.

In the beginning...

Stolen stories

The Car Man was inspired by the opera *Carmen*, a dramatic love story about a girl from a cigar factory in 19th-century Spain. The music was written by French composer Georges Bizet (1838–75). Like the opera, the ballet uses themes of love and jealousy, but the altered storyline is borrowed from a classic movie: *The Postman Always Rings Twice*. Both *The Car Man* and the movie follow the same tale of a mysterious stranger who shows up in a small town, causes trouble, and ruins lives.

Scene from a 19th-century production of *Carmen*

Music to dance to

The Car Man's music is based on a special arrangement of Bizet's opera created by Rodion Shchedrin for a short ballet, also called *Carmen*. This version, written for percussion and strings, wasn't long enough for Matthew Bourne's full-length piece, so Bourne commissioned another composer, Terry Davis, to expand it.

Car Man man

Matthew Bourne started dancing at the late age of 22. After training in London, he went on to choreograph plays and musicals. In 1987, he founded Adventures in Motion Pictures, a highly original dance troupe specializing in the quirky treatment of existing ballets, plays, and movies. Bourne's latest company, called New Adventures, was founded in 2002. Among his best-known productions are an all-male *Swan Lake*, *Nutcracker!*, *Cinderella*, *Dorian Gray*, and *Edward Scissorhands*.

The Car Man

What makes *The Car Man* different from most modern dance is that it tells a story. But this story, created by choreographer Matthew Bourne, has none of the fairy-tale atmosphere of traditional ballet. It is **a dark, gritty thriller**, set in the surroundings of a small-town garage in 1960s America. Dancing with bare feet or in work boots, the characters are very real people.

The story goes... In the small town of Harmony, a group of mechanics repairs cars at Dino's Garage. In the evenings, they relax by hanging out in the local diner with their girlfriends. Dino's wife, Lana, and her sister, Rita, both work as waitresses there. One night, a handsome stranger named Luca arrives in town and charms everyone. Dino hires Luca to work in the garage, but after a time he realizes that the newcomer is becoming far too interested in his wife. Luca also befriends a timid young mechanic, Angelo—who is bullied by everyone—and teaches him to stand up for himself. Soon there is a complicated tangle of events that rapidly leads to ruined friendships, violence, and murder.

Dino's garage

The first scene of *The Car Man* takes place in Dino's Garage, where muscled mechanics in work shirts and grubby T-shirts leap around to Bizet's music. Here, we also meet two of the story's main characters—Dino, the garage owner, and Angelo, a shy, bullied assistant.

Dynamic dancing from the mechanics

Jailbird rock

In Act Two, Angelo is arrested and jailed, framed for a crime he didn't commit. In his cell, with his hands tied together, he dances a powerful solo to express his fear and anguish. Later, he has a visit from his ex-girlfriend Rita, who tells him what really happened.

Angelo dances in jail

The day's work is over and the "car men" go wild at the diner

Jonathan Oliver as Bourne's swan, 2009

Bourne's adventures

Instead of fluttering females, Bourne's *Swan Lake* features powerful male swans dancing to Tchaikovsky's music. In his story, it's the Prince, not the swan, who longs to find freedom, and the swan, not the Prince, who does the betraying. It's this version of *Swan Lake* that appears in the story of *Billy Elliot* (see page 117). In another of his ballets, Matthew Bourne made use of a modern fairy tale, *Edward Scissorhands*, originally a highly successful movie of the 1990s. Romantic, funny, and sometimes a bit creepy, this is the story of a gentle young man, created by a crazy inventor, who has sharp scissor blades in place of fingers.

Sam Archer in the title role of *Edward Scissorhands* with Kerry Biggin as Kim, the girl he loves

Circus tricks

Cirque du Soleil (which means "Circus of the Sun") began as a small stilt-walking troupe in Quebec, Canada. As the company expanded, it combined its large-scale dance and acrobatic performances with clever staging technology and lighting effects.

Colorful costumes stored backstage at a Cirque Du Soleil production of *Saltimbanco* in Poland.

To make sure the mood of a Cirque performance isn't broken, technical staff don't go on stage during the show—the **artists move props** and shift scenery and equipment.

For many of the shows, Cirque du Soleil uses **special interactive technology** to create backgrounds (such as lakes and volcanoes) that appear to respond to the performers' movements.

Cirque du Soleil never uses recorded music—**professional musicians play live** at every performance.

More than **5,000 people work for Cirque du Soleil**—there are over 50 nationalities represented, 25 languages spoken, and at least 100 different types of job involved.

Cirque du Soleil is truly global— it not only performs all over the world, but also **funds community projects** in more than 20 countries, particularly trying to help young people and those living in poverty.

Cirque du Soleil

" To take the adventure further, step beyond its dreams... "

A unique performance company began in the 1980s in Canada. It was called Cirque du Soleil and it grew to create a **dramatic, original mix of circus and street entertainment** with breathtaking dance and acrobatics. Today, its extravagant productions tour the world.

Saltimbanco's acrobatic dancers

Totem

Based on myths from many cultures, *Totem* deals with the evolution of the human race, from the first creatures that came out of the sea, to modern humans who long to fly. Part of the stage set is a giant turtle, and some of the performers are on unicycles, or roller skates.

Performers on skates during *Totem*

Saltimbanco

A celebration of the modern city, *Saltimbanco* brings to life the streets, the buildings, the sidewalks, and most of all the huge and colorful mixture of people and cultures who try to live in harmony together.

Alegria

This is not a bright and cheerful show as the name suggests (*Alegria* is Spanish for joy)— instead, it is dark and moody. The theme is oppression—of citizens by kings and governments, of the old by the young, of the poor by the rich, and of people who are different by everyone else.

Alegria has beautiful staging and costumes

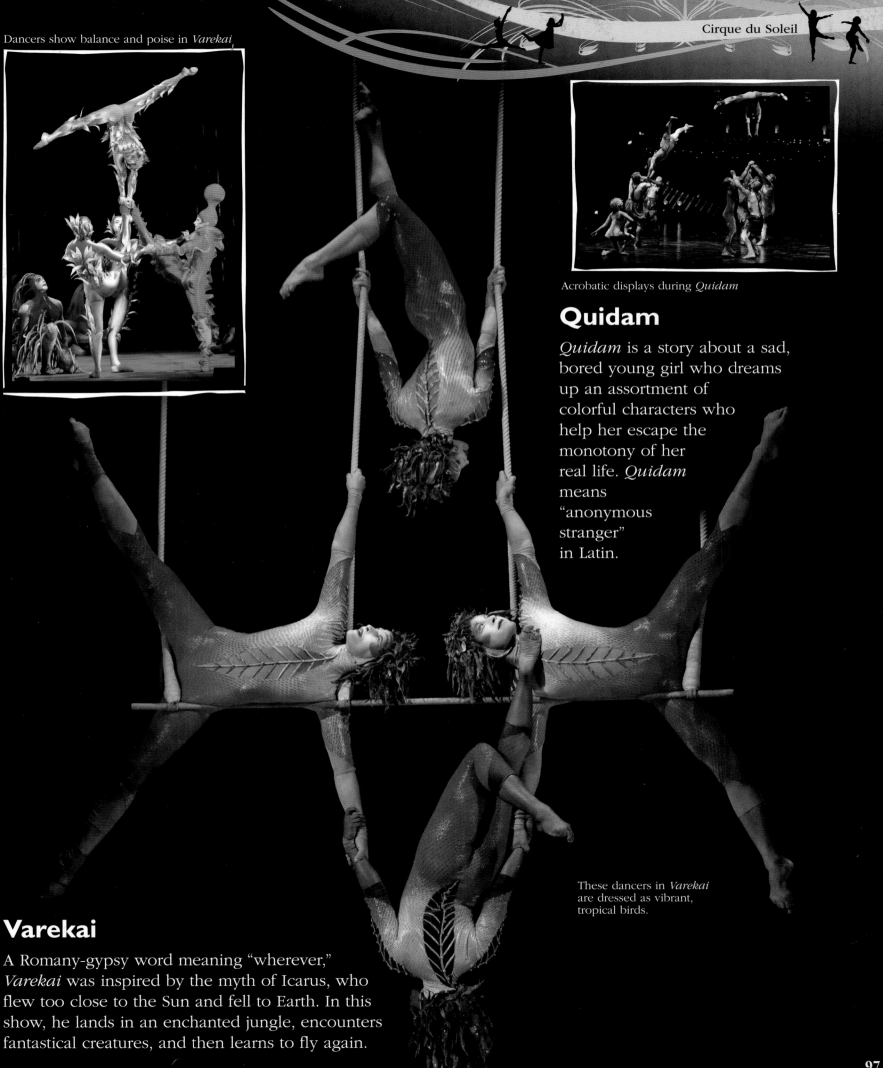

Dancers show balance and poise in *Varekai*

Acrobatic displays during *Quidam*

Quidam

Quidam is a story about a sad, bored young girl who dreams up an assortment of colorful characters who help her escape the monotony of her real life. *Quidam* means "anonymous stranger" in Latin.

These dancers in *Varekai* are dressed as vibrant, tropical birds.

Varekai

A Romany-gypsy word meaning "wherever," *Varekai* was inspired by the myth of Icarus, who flew too close to the Sun and fell to Earth. In this show, he lands in an enchanted jungle, encounters fantastical creatures, and then learns to fly again.

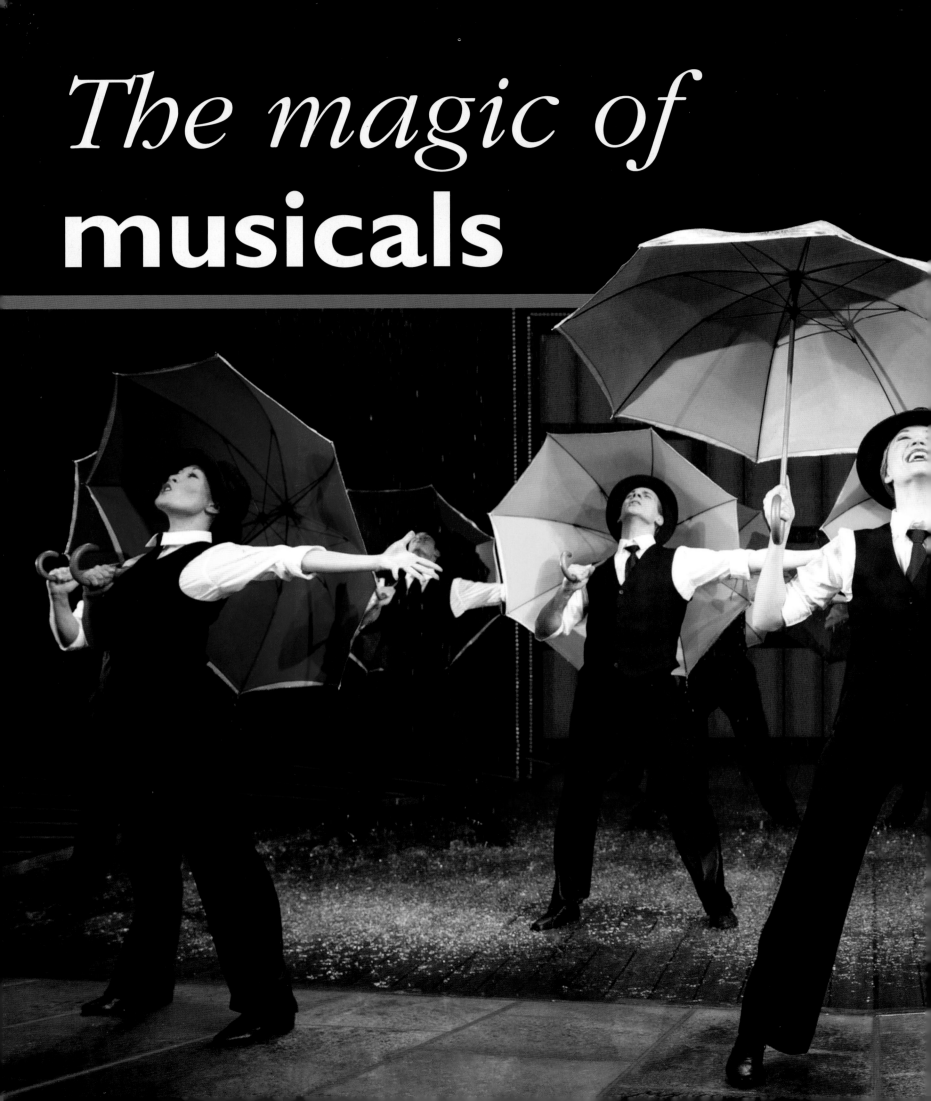

The magic of
musicals

It's hard to beat the excitement of a **glitzy musical** on stage or screen. From *Singin' in the Rain* to *High School Musical*, these spectacles of song and dance are extravaganzas of **feel-good fun**.

Show time

Until the 1920s, dancing on stage was restricted to music-hall acts and light-hearted theatrical shows. Then, in 1927, **the modern musical arrived in style** with Jerome Kern's *Show Boat*, which set the bar for future musicals. After Hollywood's silent movies became "talkies" in the 1930s, musicals soon became movie-industry fixtures. On the whole, musicals are an American and English art form, but they are enjoyed across the world.

A history of musicals

Early roots

The earliest musical dramas to feature dancing and singing were operas; a special dance section was written into many famous ones. Dancing was an important part of British music-hall and US vaudeville performances, in which an assortment of singers, dancers, musicians, jugglers, and acrobats took to the stage. Acts tended to be a series of song-and-dance sketches, with no real plot. *The Black Crook* (1866) is considered the first "musical comedy" that used song and dance to tell a story.

Music-hall performer Ella Shields

A little light relief

One of the first American musicals was George M. Cohan's *Little Johnny Jones* (1904). Cohan, himself a vaudeville star, entertained with dazzling dance routines and catchy songs. Song and dance offered a welcome escape to audiences during World War I, and comedies such as *Chu Chin Chow* (based on the Arabian Nights stories) were popular.

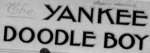

Sheet music

Theater lands

In the early 19th century, only London's "patent theaters" were allowed to stage dramatic plays. As these laws relaxed, the West End developed and the theater building boom continued until World War I. In New York City, theaters were centered on Broadway. As vaudeville developed into musicals starring high-quality singers and dancers, the district's image improved and began to attract larger audiences.

Show Boat

In 1927, the groundbreaking *Show Boat* arrived—the first full-length musical to break away from trivial plots. Composer Jerome Kern and writer Oscar Hammerstein were inspired by popular black song-and-dance shows and tackled the tough themes of race and prejudice. The song "Can't Help Lovin' Dat Man" is set to the rhythm of a black "cakewalk," and the characters, both black and white, sing and strut together.

"Can't Help Lovin' Dat Man" from the 1936 film

Movie bonanza

In the 1930s, with the arrival of "talkies" (movies with sound), Hollywood embraced musicals. With their entertaining song-and-dance formula, they were a gift to filmmakers and a big hit with audiences. Lavish musical extravaganzas with a huge cast, like those created by Busby Berkeley (see pages 102–103), could only ever exist on film.

Get in line

Most dancers in stage and screen musicals form part of the chorus line. Singing and dancing in supporting roles, they often move from one show to another. One of the most famous chorus lines in the world, though, is not part of a conventional musical—at Radio City Music Hall in New York, the chorus line (called the Rockettes) tops the bill. Every Christmas season for over a quarter of a century they've performed their perfectly precise and coordinated high-kicking routines five times a day, seven days a week, to audiences from all over the world.

Musicals at the movies

Over the decades, musicals have come in and out of movie fashion. The most successful were outstanding examples of two different styles—fresh, imaginative interpretations of stage shows (like *Oklahoma!* and *Chicago*), or movie originals created with extraordinary skill and style (like *Singin' in the Rain*).

Chicago billboard

CHICAGO

The #1 LONGEST-RUNNING AMERICAN MUSICAL in Broadway History!

TELECHARGE.COM/CHICAGO

Radio City Rockettes

Modern musicals

From their simple beginnings, musicals have developed into exciting, imaginative performances on stage and screen. Since Jerome Kern broke new theatrical ground with *Show Boat*, musicals have flourished, and today's modern hits continue to amaze audiences with roller-skating trains (*Starlight Express*), urban wildlife (*Cats*), and dancing jungle animals (*The Lion King*).

Starlight Express

Biography

1895: Born Busby Berkeley William Enos in Los Angeles, California, to theatrical parents.

1925: After working on Broadway for many years, took on his first role as dance director, on *Holka Polka*.

1927: Achieved Broadway acclaim with his work on *A Connecticut Yankee* and, the next year, *Whoopee!* with singer Eddie Cantor.

1930: Lured to Hollywood to work on the movie version of *Whoopee!*

1933: Reached the peak of his career with the release of four hit movies, including the legendary *42nd Street*.

1942: Directed Gene Kelly in his first film, *For Me and My Gal*.

1971: Supervised a revival of the 1920s musical comedy *No, No, Nanette*.

1976: Died in Palm Springs, California, at the age of 81.

Influences

On parade

As a child, Berkeley was enrolled in a military academy and then joined the army in 1918. Soon, the young lieutenant was responsible for organizing parades—formal arrangements of troops for inspection. Moving these large groups of people into, and out of, complex, geometric shapes had a big influence on Berkeley's signature style.

Soldiers marching in formation

Busby Busby Berkeley

"I wanted to make people happy, if only for an hour."

The man who invented **the most spectacular dance routines in Hollywood** never had a dance lesson in his life. Busby Berkeley's distinctive brand of production and choreography featured fun and frivolity, as well as long lines of dancers known as chorus girls.

Chorus girls in *42nd Street*

Making his mark

When Berkeley (known as "Buzz") arrived in Hollywood, dance directors had a limited role. Unhappy with this, he directed the dancers and the camera work himself. Buzz had two signature styles—he shot with a single camera and used multiple close-ups of chorus girls.

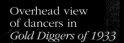
Overhead view of dancers in *Gold Diggers of 1933*

Take it from the top

The most recognizable Berkeley numbers are shot from a unique bird's-eye view. He worked on a grand scale, using many dancers to create patterns that were inspired by everything from kaleidoscope shapes to flowers.

In *Footlight Parade*, Berkeley used mirrors and hundreds of dancers

The beat of dancing feet

In the early 1930s, during a time of extreme hardship called the Great Depression, people needed cheering up, and Berkeley did just that. For the movie *42nd Street*, he was hired to direct the musical numbers. The film, about a talented understudy who gets a chance to perform, painted a gritty picture of backstage life. Its message that hard work and perseverance pay off, together with Berkeley's magic, made the movie a huge hit with audiences.

42nd Street

Busby in Hollywood

After the success of *42nd Street*, Berkeley stayed on in Hollywood and worked with a number of stars including swimming actress Esther Williams, whose amazing water ballets he arranged in aqua-musicals. By the end of the 1930s, the overblown musical had fallen out of fashion. However, in 1942, Berkeley directed a low-key comedy called *For Me and My Gal*, with newcomer Gene Kelly. Kelly turned out to be a fantastic dancer and was destined to be star.

Esther Williams in *Million Dollar Mermaid*

103

In the beginning...

Tap roots

During the 1800s, people from all over the world crossed the ocean to the United States and brought music and dance with them. They included farmers and laborers escaping poverty in Ireland, England, and Scotland. Also among these people were slaves, captured and transported from Africa. Dancing and drumming were important in African culture, but many slaves were forbidden to play their traditional drums, so they banged out rhythms with their feet instead. This "step" dancing spread and blended with other cultural dances such as the Irish jig and English clog dancing. The combined style, which came to be known as "buck and wing," was the beginning of tap.

Bill Robinson with Shirley Temple

Mr. Bojangles

"Minstrel" revues, in which both black and white men imitated slaves dancing, were the first public shows to feature early forms of tap. One performer who began his career in similar revues, Bill "Bojangles" Robinson, went on to become America's most famous tap dancer. By the 1920s he was dancing on Broadway. Then, during the early 1930s, he forged a successful movie career in Hollywood, appearing with child superstar Shirley Temple. Bill Robinson's birthday, May 25, is the official National Tap Dance Day in the United States.

Happy tapping

Tap is sometimes called America's unofficial national dance. Brought to life by African slaves on Southern plantations, tap is a mixture of **steps, jigs, and rhythms** from different cultures. This dance form has moved on a long way from its roots, first on to the stage and then into movies, becoming part of the country's performance heritage.

Into the mainstream

By the time "Mr. Bojangles" (see left) reached Hollywood in the 1930s, tap was part of the mainstream musical. Busby Berkeley (see pages 102–03) used tap in his fabulous productions, and the next generation of dance stars made it their own. The Nicholas Brothers mixed tap with acrobatics; Eleanor Powell added high kicks and splits; Fred Astaire blended tap with ballroom moves; and Gene Kelly's version was balletic but athletic. Tap began to be seen as two styles: "rhythm" tap, with loose, intricate footwork, and "show," or "Broadway" tap, with bigger arm and body movements.

Eleanor Powell tapping in the movie musical *Broadway Melody of 1938*

Sammy Davis Jr.

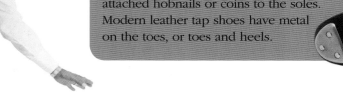

Shoes with sound

Footwear that makes a noise is nothing new. In ancient Rome, dancers nailed pieces of metal called *scabilla* to their sandals. At one time in Europe, an important part of country dancing in working-class communities was the sound of the wooden clogs that people wore. In 19th-century America, early tap shoes had wooden soles. When lighter leather shoes came in, dancers attached hobnails or coins to the soles. Modern leather tap shoes have metal on the toes, or toes and heels.

Keeping it going

When the big 1940s and 50s musicals fell out of fashion, tap went quiet, too. However, the spirit of tap was kept alive by all-around performers such as Gregory Hines and Sammy Davis Jr. Hines danced in a 1989 film, *Tap*, wearing electronic tap shoes connected to synthesizers—so when he tapped he created a whole range of different sounds.

Funky footwork

Today, tap is hugely popular. Its revival, which began in the 1980s, is largely due to the brilliant dancer and choreographer Savion Glover, a pupil of Gregory Hines (see left). Glover took tap back to its African roots, making it young and funky. His style is hard and loud, with an emphasis on what he calls "hitting"—saying something through the steps. Glover's rhythms and moves are true to the spirit of tap. He works in television and film, and creates spectacular stage dances.

Savion Glover was a choreographer for the penguin tap sequences in the movie *Happy Feet*

The *Tap Dogs* team on stage

Dancing Dogs

One of the most famous brands of tap in recent decades appeared in Australia, when dancer and choreographer Dein Perry created his *Tap Dogs*. First seen in 1995, this unique 80-minute show features men dressed as construction workers, performing nonstop tap routines on an elaborate construction-site set. *Tap Dogs* was so popular that variations of the original Sydney show are now performed all over the world.

The golden age

Big musicals had their golden years, on both stage and screen, throughout the 1940s and 50s. As tastes in entertainment changed, the musical was pushed aside, but it never disappeared altogether. New **song and dance shows**—and fresh versions of the old favorites—continue to delight each generation.

▲ **Oklahoma! (1943)** The show is set in the American Midwest in the 1900s. Romance and rivalry are stirring up trouble between farmers and cowboys. When Rodgers and Hammerstein's *Oklahoma!* opened on Broadway, audiences loved the music and drama. Agnes de Mille, pioneer of dance with an American setting, was the choreographer. "The Farmer and the Cowman" (above, in the 1955 movie) is a riotous number that ends in a fight.

▶ **An American in Paris (1951)**
This movie stars two highly trained dancers—Gene Kelly, as a struggling painter, and Leslie Caron, as the girl he loves. *An American in Paris* was inspired by George Gershwin's musical composition of the same name. The dance routines, choreographed by Kelly, are all set to Gershwin's music.

▶ **West Side Story (1957)** This is Romeo and Juliet (see pages 76–77) moved to New York City, where two rival gangs, the Jets and the Sharks, rule the streets. Music by Leonard Bernstein and dances by Jerome Robbins made it a stage hit. In the 1961 movie, right, "Shark" girl Anita (Rita Moreno) leads the number "America."

Hello, Dolly! (1964) Dolly is a widow whose life's work is matching up couples and hoping they'll fall in love. She's also eager to find a new husband for herself. Originally a hit stage show on Broadway, *Hello, Dolly!* was made into a movie in 1969. Both words and music of this light-hearted musical are by Jerry Herman. The show-stopping highlight is the title song and dance number "Hello, Dolly!," performed here by Barbara Streisand, star of the movie.

Top Hat (1935) This was the most successful movie pairing of famous dance team Fred Astaire and Ginger Rogers. Designer clothes, luxury hotels, and Venetian canals set the scene, while the lead couple sort out mistaken identities, overcome romantic difficulties, and dance elegantly to Irving Berlin's score. During the filming of the "Cheek to Cheek" number (see below), Astaire got covered with ostrich feathers from Rogers' glamorous dress.

A Chorus Line (1975) Auditioning for work in a Broadway musical, a mixed bunch of chorus dancers take turns telling their private stories. The show ends with a polished stage routine performed by the chosen few (above). *A Chorus Line* was choreographed for Broadway by Michael Bennett, with music by Marvin Hamlisch. A movie version appeared in 1985.

Cats (1981) Based on a collection of amusing poems about cats written by T. S. Eliot, this musical was a surprising success. With its magical dances, stunning costumes, and a large cast of various "cat" characters, the show won a place in the history of musicals. Andrew Lloyd Webber wrote the score and Gillian Lynne created the dances.

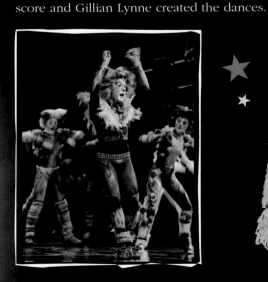

In the beginning...

Not a new song

The song "Singin' in the Rain" was not specially written for the movie, but had been a popular tune since the late 1920s. The lyrics were written by Arthur Freed, a producer at the MGM film studios, and the music by composer Nacio Herb Brown. These two had produced many other hit songs that were used in movies. "Singin' in the Rain" itself featured in six different films.

Cast members of *The Hollywood Revue* (1929)—in which the song "Singin' in the Rain" made its debut

Hollywood history

The plot of *Singin' in the Rain*, which tells how Hollywood moved from silent movies into "talkies," is based on fact and, in some cases, on real people. The writers, a husband-and-wife team, may have been thinking about the former owner of their house when they wrote their script. He was a one-time star of the silent screen who lost his job, money, and fame when recorded sound arrived.

Top talent

The star of *Singin' in the Rain* was the multitalented Gene Kelly, an American actor, singer, and dancer. Kelly not only had a share in directing the film, but he also produced all the choreography. Sharing top billing with Kelly were music-hall song-and-dance man Donald O'Connor and 19-year-old newcomer, Debbie Reynolds.

Gene Kelly and Debbie Reynolds in a publicity still for the film.

Singin' *in the Rain*

The 1952 poster of *Singin' in the Rain*

Some of the **best-loved dance numbers in musical history** feature in the movie *Singin' in the Rain*, first screened in 1952. Unusually, this musical includes hardly any original songs—most were collected from earlier films and shows, and the writers had to weave the plot around them.

The story goes... Don Lockwood (Gene Kelly) is a silent-movie star who is in the middle of making the film, *The Dueling Cavalier*. To boost publicity, his movie studio, Monumental, tries to encourage a romance between Don and his leading lady, Lina Lamont (Jean Hagen). When a rival studio releases the first sound movie, Monumental has no choice but to turn the film into a talkie, but there's a problem. Don's voice is fine, but Lina's is harsh and unpleasant. Don, helped by his best friend Cosmo Brown (Donald O'Connor), tries to replace Lina with a talented chorus girl Kathy Seldon (Debbie Reynolds), with whom he is already half in love. Their developing romance, the plotting involved in the change of cast, and the making of a silent movie into a musical, provide the film's story and the perfect setting for its unique songs and dances.

One of the movie's high points is the number "Make 'Em Laugh," danced by Cosmo. In the acrobatic, slapstick routine, Cosmo runs up a wall and does a somersault. When the scene was finished, after multiple takes, the exhausted O'Connor was bedridden for days. Unfortunately, the original footage was accidentally destroyed, so O'Connor had to do it all again.

"Good Mornin'"—Debbie Reynolds' big moment

Cyd Charisse with Kelly in "Broadway Melody"

Star making

Singin' in the Rain not only made a star of Debbie Reynolds, but the movie also helped the career of the relatively unknown Cyd Charisse, chosen by Gene Kelly as his partner for the final number, "Broadway Melody."

Rain, rain

Gene Kelly's splashy dance along a rainy street is the key moment of the movie. Starry-eyed and smitten after he kisses Kathy goodnight, Don gets out his umbrella, sets off for home, and loses himself in his song, "Singin' in the Rain." Apparently, when this scene was shot, Kelly was running a high fever, and the hosed "rain" soaked right through to his skin.

To make the "rain" of the title song easier to see, the hosed water was mixed with milk

On the boards

In 1983, a West End production of *Singin' in the Rain* opened in London, followed two years later by a Broadway version in New York. New productions continue to be staged to the present day, with an unchanged plot and all the music from the movie—classics such as "Good Morning," "Make 'em Laugh," "Broadway Melody," and the legendary "Singin' in the Rain"—plus an assortment of additional songs. Stylish choreography, elaborate sets, and great performances ensure that the stage version has all the the charm, romance, comedy, and the all-round "feel-good" factor of the original movie.

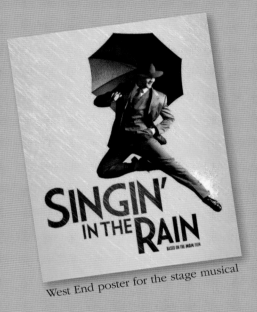

West End poster for the stage musical

Stage showers

As in the movie, the highlight of the stage version is the puddle-strewn "Singin' in the Rain" number, complete with an on-stage shower. Thousands of gallons of falling water, and special staging and lighting, give the effect of a "flooded stage." During the song, the orchestra and the first few rows of the audience are routinely drenched.

The cast of *Singin' in the Rain* at London's Palace Theatre splash about as the "rain" pours down

Biography

1927: Born in Chicago, Illinois, the son of music-hall performer Cyril Fosse.

1950: Appeared in his first Broadway show, *Dance Me a Song*.

1954: Choreographed *The Pajama Game* on Broadway, and followed it the next year with *Damn Yankees*.

1966: Directed and choreographed *Sweet Charity* for his wife, Broadway star Gwen Verdon.

1972: Directed the movie version of the stage musical *Cabaret*.

1973: Triple award winner for *Cabaret* (Oscar for Best Director), *Pippin* (Tony for Best Musical Director), and *Liza with a Z* (a Liza Minnelli special for which he received an Emmy for Best Musical Director).

1975: Choreographed the revolutionary gangster stage musical *Chicago*.

1979: Wrote, directed, and choreographed *All That Jazz*, a largely autobiographical movie.

1987: Died in Washington, D.C.

Influences

Tread like Fred

Bob Fosse's earliest influence, and his life-long hero, was actor and dancer Fred Astaire. Fosse moved to New York to follow in his idol's dance steps. Astaire's apparently relaxed and fluid style of movement, and his use of props like chairs and hats, all appeared in Fosse's later work.

Bob *Fosse*

❝ *Live like you'll die tomorrow…
and dance like nobody's watching.* ❞

In the **world of musical theater and film dance**, few people have had more impact than Bob Fosse. Dancer, actor, choreographer, and director, he created a style of dance that was teasing, entertaining, and always cool. His work won him three major award in one year.

Warming up

Bob Fosse's first try at choreography was a number for a local nightclub, featuring girls with ostrich-feather fans. In 1945, toward the end of World War II, he joined the US Navy and was sent to entertain the troops. Later, he moved to New York City, and in 1950 he appeared on Broadway in a revue (variety show) called *Dance Me a Song*. Soon after, he tried his luck in Hollywood and was given a small dance role in the movie version of *Kiss Me Kate* in 1953.

Bob Fosse and Carol Haney in *Kiss Me Kate*

First steps

In 1954 Fosse choreographed a hit Broadway musical, *The Pajama Game*, which was about a workers' dispute in a factory. He went on to win an award for the baseball-themed *Damn Yankees*. On this project he met Gwen Verdon, his wife and dance partner, who inspired two other Broadway hits: *Redhead* and *Sweet Charity*. *The Pajama Game*, *Damn Yankees*, and *Sweet Charity* were all made into successful movies.

Movie poster for *Sweet Charity*, 1968

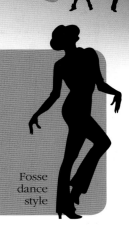

Life is a cabaret

Perhaps the best-loved Fosse project is the 1972 movie *Cabaret*, based on a Broadway stage production. The story is set in Berlin in the 1930s, a time when the Nazis were rising to power. Fosse directed and choreographed the movie. He altered much of the original stage show and reset nearly all the musical numbers in a nightclub, where the star turn is good-time girl Sally Bowles (Liza Minnelli).

Liza Minnelli strikes a pose in this 1972 movie poster of *Cabaret*

Full-time Fosse

Most dancers keep their tummies tucked in, backs straight, shoulders down, and legs turned out, but Bob Fosse was different. He danced with hips forward, shoulders rounded, arms hanging, and knees bent and slightly turned in. To hide his thinning hair and his hands, which he didn't like, Fosse wore hats and gloves. His influence on the style of younger dancers like Michael Jackson (see pages 134–135) is clear.

Fosse dance style

Typical Fosse

The show that best reflects Fosse's style is *Chicago*. Set in the 1920s, it is the story of two jailed murderesses who battle for instant fame. Fosse choreographed the 1975 stage show against his typical backdrop of semi-realistic settings and dramatic lighting. While *Chicago* showcases Fosse's work, his life story, barely disguised, is told in the 1979 film *All That Jazz*, which Fosse wrote, directed, and choreographed.

The "jazz hands" gesture is a Fosse favorite

The London cast of *Chicago*

Bollywood magic

Inspired by the name Hollywood, Bollywood refers to the Hindi-language movie industry that is based in Bombay (now Mumbai), India. Bollywood movies are mostly musicals, and contain **spectacular song-and-dance routines** as an integral part of the plot.

▲ **Kashmir ki Kali (1964)** In the song "Tarif Karun Kya Uski," Shammi Kapoor sways and claps in a *shikara* (boat) on Dal Lake, Kashmir. Kapoor was known as the "Elvis Presley of India" for his frenetic and lively dancing style.

▶ **Dil Se (1998)** The song "Chaiyya Chaiyya" was unique in that it was shot entirely on top of a moving train. Set to Oscar-winning composer A. R. Rahman's catchy music, the song was filmed in Ooty, Tamil Nadu, and featured superstar Shah Rukh Khan and actress Malaika Arora. The rustic dance moves are based on Indian folk dances.

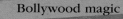

▶ Kabhi Khushi Kabhie Gham (2001)

Starring heart-throb Hrithik Roshan—considered one of the best dancers in Bollywood—the song "Deewana Hai Dekho" features dazzling leaps and energetic dance moves. Shown here is Roshan and his dancers in the British Museum, London—the first time any movie sequence had been shot there.

◀ Devdas (2002)

Madhuri Dixit's exquisite rendition of "Maar Dala" is one of the best *mujra* (courtesan) dances in Hindi movie history. Infused with classical beats and *thumkas* (hip movements), the dance was inspired by the graceful classical dances of India. Dixit was choreographed by the legendary Saroj Khan against a stunning backdrop, one of the biggest and most expensive Bollywood sets ever built.

◀ Om Shanti Om (2007)

The song "Dhoom Tana" features Deepika Padukone, who mesmerized the audience with her classical moves. She used *hasta mudras* (hand gestures), an element of Indian classical dance. The multiple arms around Padukone (see left) belong to dancers standing behind her in a row.

▲ Tees Maar Khan (2010)

"Sheila ki Jawani" is a sizzling number danced by actress Katrina Kaif in the movie *Tees Maar Khan*. She combined both Arabic and contemporary dance steps and trained under a belly-dancing expert to master her hip-shaking moves.

▶ The Merchants of Bollywood (2010)

A spectacular Australian dance musical, The *Merchants of Bollywood* charts the history of the Hindi movie industry. Choreographed by Vaibhavi Merchant, an ensemble of performers dressed in vibrant, traditional costumes dance energetically to a fusion of Western and Indian dance forms.

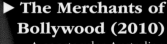

Bollywood steps

Song-and-dance sequences are a key part of Bollywood movies and a huge hit with audiences. The **dancing and choreography of popular songs** is widely copied and performed at weddings, festivals, and other events.

"Singing and smiling add energy to our dance."
Shrina, Nikita, Natasha

Influences

The dancing in early Bollywood movies drew heavily from folk and classical dances from all across India. Although the dances today are modern, a wide variety of influences come into play.

Eye contact with the audience is important

Dances in early Bollywood movies borrow movements from South Indian classical dances, such as bharatanatyam, which involves lots of exquisite poses and hand gestures.

Traditional

Bharatanatyam

Traditional Bollywood dance focuses on acting out the lyrics of the song, which is often part of the story and usually relates to love and marriage (see panel right).

▼ Matching steps

Since Bollywood dance numbers are often performed in groups, the dancers must practice doing the same moves at the same time.

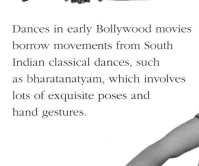

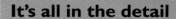

Kathak

Classical kathak dance was first danced in Uttar Pradesh, a state in northern India. This dance style involves complex footwork and intricate hand movements.

Arabic

Arabic dance from the Middle East is a more recent influence on Bollywood dancing. It takes a lot of stamina and involves quick vibrating movements like belly dancing.

Folk

Folk dances of India usually appear in festival or celebration scenes. In the dandiya dance, performers move around hitting dandiyas (sticks). This type of dance is mostly seen at Gujarati celebrations.

Bhangra

Based on traditional Punjabi folk dances, bhangra has a strong dhol drum beat. The movements are energetic, involving raised arms and lots of jumping and kicking.

It's all in the detail

Facial expressions

Because of its origins in movies, Bollywood dance requires a great deal of acting. The song lyrics are often part of the story—falling in love, getting married, or celebrating events and festivals. This means that the characters' facial expressions need to reflect their emotions when they dance, to show happiness, excitement, shyness, or sadness. Many dances are centered around weddings, and dance moves often show the bride getting ready, putting on jewelry and makeup.

Putting on bangles

Bride-to-be expressing shyness

Hand gestures

Hand gestures are an important detail, since they bring so much expression to Bollywood dancing. Dancers need to keep practicing to make sure the fingers and arms are in the right position and at the correct angle at all times.

Fingers stretched out wide

Hands facing each other

Thumb and fingers brought together

Arm outstretched with elbow bent

Teen dreams

During the 1950s, there was a dramatic change in Western society—teenagers were invented! Previously, girls and boys in their teens were seen as unfinished adults, without their own tastes and opinions. Then rock and roll burst into being, and **teenage culture was born**. Since the 1970s, many hit movies and stage shows, set in various decades, tell the story of young people dancing their way to self-discovery.

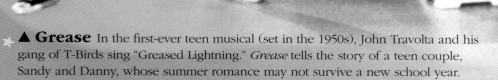

▲ Grease In the first-ever teen musical (set in the 1950s), John Travolta and his gang of T-Birds sing "Greased Lightning." *Grease* tells the story of a teen couple, Sandy and Danny, whose summer romance may not survive a new school year.

▲ Dirty Dancing
On vacation with her family at a mountain resort, Frances ("Baby") falls in love with the resident dance instructor. Above, in the leading roles, Patrick Swayze and Jennifer Grey show off their ballroom style.

▶ Hairspray
Tracy (Nikki Blonsky, right) uses dance to fight prejudice, directed at her (because of her weight) and her friends (because they're black). Set in the 1960s, the film reflects attitudes that were common at the time.

▶ **Fame** This movie follows the lives of students at the New York High School of Performing Arts. The young dancers seen here are going wild to the title song. They discover that "Fame costs—and right here is where you start paying..."

▲ **Flashdance** Alex (played by Jennifer Beals) works as a welder in a steel mill but at night she dances in a bar. She longs to be accepted at a well-known dance school. The movie tells her story of tragedy and eventual triumph.

▶ **Footloose** In the small Rocky Mountain town of Bomont, dancing has been banned. When city boy Ren (Kevin Bacon in the film) arrives, he joins forces with a feisty local girl named Ariel to get the ban lifted, so their high school can have a senior prom.

◀ **Billy Elliot** Set in the North of England during a miners' strike, *Billy Elliot* tells the story of a boy who stumbles into a ballet class by accident. He discovers a hidden talent and secretly dreams of becoming a dancer. In the stage version (shown left), Billy is played by Liam Mower.

In the beginning...

Original TV movie

Released by the Disney Channel as a movie for television in 2006, the original *High School Musical* was watched by 7.7 million people on its first viewing—the channel's highest figure for any movie that year. Although the story is set in the fictional East High School in Albequerque, New Mexico, much of the movie was filmed in a real-life East High School in Salt Lake City, Utah.

Soundtrack

It took a team of 12 people to write the movie's music. The soundtrack went on to become the best-selling album in the US in the year the movie was released.

Family tree

Originally the story of *High School Musical* was intended as the plot of *Grease 3* (see pages 116–117). Troy and Gabriella would have been the children of Sandy and Danny, and Sharpay would have been the daughter of Betty Rizzo.

High-school industry

The *High School Musical* series was hugely successful and has become a globally popular brand. It went on to inspire international versions of the movie in Argentina and Brazil, plus a concert tour, a stage musical (see right), an ice-skating tour, and a reality-TV series. There is plenty of merchandise, too: T-shirts, books, video games posters, and even playing cards.

High School Musical playing cards

High School *Musical*

Meeting for the first time

This feel-good story about a group of teenagers is packed with appealing stars, engaging songs and dances, and encouragement to **follow your dreams**. *High School Musical* has attracted record-breaking audiences all over the world.

The story goes... At a ski lodge, strangers Troy and Gabriella are pushed into a karaoke duet. They discover they sing well together, and exchange numbers. When Troy goes back to school, he finds that Gabriella has moved to the same city, and enrolled at the same school. Troy is the star basketball player, and Gabriella is a serious student, but they're both tempted to audition for the nerdy school musical. They have to battle the ambitious Sharpay, as well as their classmates who fear that the pair's attraction to music—and each other—will turn them away from their friends and interests. The two get together, win parts in the show, and everyone is happy.

Get'cha Head in the Game

Grace and movement

In one of the movie's most impressive dance numbers "Get'cha Head in the Game," Troy and the Wildcats basketball team sing about the importance of concentration while they toss the ball around the court. Their bounces, dribbles, and runs turn into dance steps, and the practice session becomes polished choreography, highlighting control, coordination, and teamwork. Before the movie began shooting, the whole cast was given intensive dance training, and the boys had to be coached in basketball skills as well.

Man behind the moves

High School Musical was choreographed and directed by Kenny Ortega, who worked on Madonna's video "Material Girl" in 1985 and created the choreography for *Dirty Dancing* (see page 116). During the 1990s, he worked with Michael Jackson (see pages 134–135) on the Dangerous and HIStory tours, and was working with the singer on his comeback project "This Is It" when the singer died. Ortega was involved in the *High School Musical* project from the beginning, and created the sequels.

Stars of *High School Musical*

High School sequels

High School Musical 2

The success of *High School Musical* led to two sequels, both featuring the same leading actors. *High School Musical 2* (2007) achieved even higher viewing figures than the original. This story involves Troy, Gabriella, their friends, and the Wildcats preparing for a summer talent show. Sharpay attempts to steal Troy and sabotage her rivals, though all ends happily.

High School Musical 3

High School Musical 3

The third installment—*High School Musical 3: Senior Year* (2008)—was shown in cinemas rather than on television, setting a record for the highest-ever box-office takings on its first weekend of release. This time the students of East High stage a theatrical project in their final year and wonder what they'll do now that school is over.

On stage

The stage version of the show followed the film. It appeared on New York's Broadway and London's West End, as well as around the world. Amateur versions are very popular in schools, too.

High School Musical on stage in London

Breakin' and street

Fresh dance styles came from the streets and clubs of the US, inspired by **disco, funk, and hip-hop** music. Made popular by stars such as Michael Jackson, street dance is now a global phenomenon.

Breakin' out

How it all started

On the streets of the Bronx, New York City, in the 1970s, a whole new music tradition—hip-hop—was born. Soon, it had **its own dance style**, in which performers improvised spectacular athletic routines. Breakin' began on street corners and at block parties—now it's on stages and screens around the world.

Disco dance music
Challenging popular rock music, disco had begun to take over the charts from the mid-1970s onward. Nightclubs in the US and Europe were full of disco-dancing divas enjoying the funk-, Latin-, and soul-influenced sounds.

James Brown
The 1972 hit "Get on the Good Foot" by funk and soul singer James Brown gave rise to a new dance craze called "The Good Foot." This trend in turn influenced many "breakers" (see box below) in their early development.

James Brown

DJ Kool Herc
Widely credited with developing the "break beat" in the early 1970s, DJ Kool Herc used two turntables to extend the instrumental part of records at block parties in the Bronx. The loop gave dancers more time to shine.

Putting the "B" in B-boy
The Bronx and Brooklyn dancers would go wild during the instrumental "break" in a song, dancing in their own hip-hop style. They became known as "breakers," or "breakboys" and "breakgirls," or "B-boys" and "B-girls."

Funk styles
Meanwhile, on the West Coast, in California, the funk styles of locking and popping evolved, pioneered by The Lockers and The Electric Boogaloos. Both styles appeared on the legendary TV show *Soul Train* during the 1970s, which helped to spread their popularity.

Soul Train dancers

The birth of MTV
In 1981, Music Television (MTV) was born. It instantly provided a global platform for the street dance styles that began to be used in "3-minute movies" to promote music. In 1983, Michael Jackson's widely loved 14-minute music video "Thriller" was released and became massively well-known, marking a turning point for the music video. During the 1980s and '90s, a broad range of street dance styles were featured in music videos, making MTV even more popular and spreading these dance styles all around the world.

B-boy style
Breakin' moves included toprock (floorwork), uprock (standing), power moves, and freezes (holding poses), demonstrated during "battles" by single dancers or crews (see pages 132–33).

"Wild Style"

Two movies in 1983 showcased street dance: *Wild Style* was about hip-hop culture and dance, and *Flashdance* was the first mainstream Hollywood movie to feature breakdancing. Crazy Legs and Mr. Wiggles from the Rock Steady Crew feature in the movie as dancers.

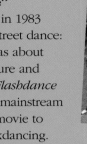

Battle of the Year

In 1990, Germany held Battle of the Year—one of the first street dance competitions. B-Boy Summit and Freestyle Session (US), UK B-Boy Championships (UK), The Notorious IBE (Netherlands), Juste Debout (France), and R16 Korea (South Korea) soon followed.

Tommy the Clown

Thomas Johnson created "clowning" (see page 131) in the early 1990s, which was danced to hip-hop music. The style evolved into the rawer dance form "krumping."

Television talent contests

Talent competitions such as the US show *So You Think You Can Dance* brought hip-hop dance to an even bigger audience—eventually the show was made in 22 different countries. In 2008, Randy Jackson launched *America's Best Dance Crew* on MTV, making crews such as Jabbawockeez and Quest Crew famous. In Europe, street dancers Salah and B-Boy Junior won the French talent show *Incroyable Talent*, and George Sampson and the crew Diversity won *Britain's Got Talent* in the UK.

In the house

In 2007, House Dance International was established in New York City. It is a festival that celebrates house, waacking, vogueing, and other dance styles that came originally from house and electronic music in Chicago and New York in the 1970s.

On the Rize

Two extraordinary documentaries featuring street dance were made in the 2000s. In 2005, David LaChapelle's movie *Rize* documented the story of clowning and krumping, and in 2007, *Planet B-Boy* traced the history of breakin'.

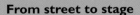

Breakin' into movies

Many films with plots centered around street dance were made in the 2000s, including: two *Save the Last Dance* movies (2001, 2006), *Honey (2003)* and *Honey 2 (2011)*, *You Got Served (2004)* and *You Got Served: Beat the World* (2011), four *Step Up* movies (2006, 2008, 2010, 2012), and two *Street Dance 3-D* movies (2010, 2012).

Online, Jon M. Chu created a unique web series called *The Legion of Extraordinary Dancers,* also known as *The LXD*. It is a story of good versus evil, where each dancer's individual skill becomes his superpower. *The LXD* showcases some of the world's best dance talent.

From street to stage

Over the last 40 years, street dance has moved on from its improvised roots—it now features in choreographed, mainstream entertainment shows. In 2008, the first ever hip-hop dance show on London's West End, *Into the Hoods*, also became the longest-running dance show on the West End stage. The show, an urban fairy tale, was created by ZooNation Dance Company, and its success has highlighted the popularity of "dance theater" shows.

Into the Hoods Rowen Hawkins

The LXD online series

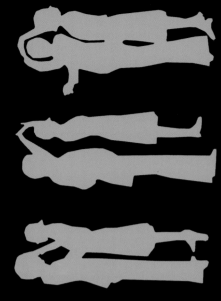
Steps for the hustle

Friday night disco at Studio 54, New York

Disco fever

During the 1970s, a new style of dance music called "disco" grew up in American cities such as New York and Philadelphia. This new sound, with its catchy vocals and powerful beat, **encouraged everyone to get up and dance,** and inspired the worldwide spread of special dance clubs called "discotheques."

The disco sound

The disco sound has funk, soul, and Latin roots, mixed with electronics using complex production technology. Strings, horns, and keyboards provide the background to individual singers and groups. The best-known disco performers of the 1970s include Donna Summer (the "Queen of Disco"), The Bee Gees, Gloria Gaynor, Chic, and The Jackson 5 (later The Jacksons).

Do the hustle

Inspired by 1950s swing dancing and Latin styles such as samba and cha-cha-cha, disco dances were either solo dances, partner dances, or dances such as the Hustle, which was a popular disco dance that was really a simplified form of line dancing (see pages 50–51). It has a set sequence of steps that are repeated, with a slight change of direction built in.

Disco inferno

By the late 1970s, most cities had a disco scene. Specialized DJs produced a smooth mix of music so that clubbers could keep dancing all night. These clubs often had slick lighting systems that throbbed on and off to the beat, dark or mirrored walls, sparkly glitterballs on the ceiling, and smoky dry ice for atmosphere. Women wore floaty dresses and high heels, while men chose close-fitting pants and tight shiny shirts, opened to show off their medallions.

Gloria Gaynor

Disco band Chic

Night fever

The movie that turned disco into a worldwide phenomenon was 1977's *Saturday Night Fever*. The story is centered on Brooklyn teenager Tony Manero (played by John Travolta), who lives in a poor neighborhood, has a boring job in a paint store, and is unhappy at home. However, he comes to life every Saturday night when his stylish dance moves make him the star of the local discotheque, 2001 Odyssey. The movie made millions, and the Bee Gees' soundtrack album was one of the most successful of all time. Songs like "Stayin' Alive," "Jive Talkin," "Night Fever," and "Disco Inferno" provided a soundtrack for the lives of a whole generation.

Funk styles and *breakin'*

In the 1970s, **dance exploded on to the streets** of the US, with two different styles on each side of the country. On the West Coast, the funk styles of locking and popping evolved in California, pioneered by The Lockers and The Electric Boogaloos. On the East Coast, it was all about b-boying and the Rock Steady Crew.

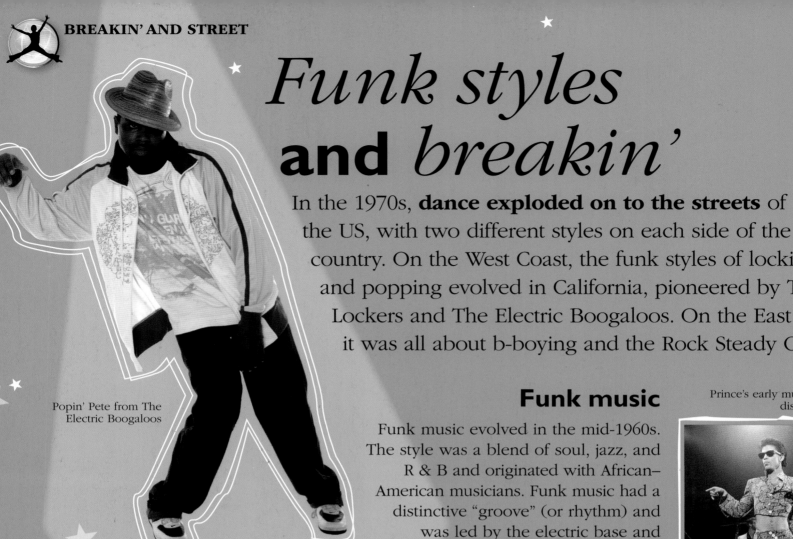

Popin' Pete from The Electric Boogaloos

Funk music

Funk music evolved in the mid-1960s. The style was a blend of soul, jazz, and R & B and originated with African–American musicians. Funk music had a distinctive "groove" (or rhythm) and was led by the electric base and drums. James Brown was one of those who started the sound, and later artists such as Prince put their distinctive spin on it. Afrika Bambaataa developed electro funk in 1982, which was more synthesizer driven. Dance crazes soon followed these new sounds.

Prince's early music blended disco and funk

Popping and locking

The funk styles of popping and locking are often confused, but they are two very different techniques. Popping is the rapid contraction and release of muscles, so it appears that they are exploding or "popping" out of the skin. Tutting, strobing, ticking, dime-stopping, waving, and electric boogaloo are styles and techniques within this genre. Locking was originally called "Campbellocking" after its creator, Don Campbell. It combines short, sharp moves with "locks," or pauses, all synchronized to the music.

Singer Kid Creole wearing a zoot suit

Funky fashions

Fashion trends for lockers and poppers varied over the years. Lockers often had a very distinctive snappy style, such as the zoot suit worn with retro alligator-look shoes. They also wore T-shirts with baggy pants that stopped at the knee, striped socks, white gloves, and large, soft "apple-boy" caps.

Grandmaster Flash at his turntables

From disco and funk to break beats

In the early 1970s in the Bronx, New York City, DJ Kool Herc developed the technique of playing two copies of the same record (most often funk or disco records), using two turntables, and switching between them—extending the "break," or rhythmic section, of the record. This was called the "break beat." Herc would talk rhythmically over the top of the breaks—an early example of rapping. The break beat technique was later made popular by Afrika Bambaataa and Grandmaster Flash.

B-boys and B-girls

A "Breaker" was someone who danced to the break beat in the music. Breakers became known as B-boys and B-girls. The dance style originated in the suburbs of the Bronx and Brooklyn in the late 1970s. Breakers developed uprock (standing), toprock (floorwork), power moves, and suicides (dangerous-looking flips) when competing on their own, as duos, or as part of a crew.

Performing a power move

A B-boy "battle"

What is "battling"?

A dance "battle" can take place on a street corner, at a nightclub, or on stage in front of an audience. Traditionally, each competitor or crew stands opposite the other and takes turns demonstrating their skills. Battles can be in any style—B-boying, popping, locking, house, krump, or new style. The winner is decided by a panel of judges or by the reaction of the crowd.

Adidas Superstar 80s

B-boy clothing

A big part of B-boy and B-girl culture is the clothing. In the 1980s, nylon tracksuits and Adidas "shell toe" sneakers (above) were worn by breakers. Today, casual clothing is worn plus lightweight sneakers with a good grip.

B-boying

Learning how to be a B-boy takes a lot of training and discipline. Moves require **upper-body strength and good balance**. Poses are acrobatic but they need to look graceful, too. Many beginners wear knee, elbow, and head pads to protect their bodies.

"My style? I like to mix it up a bit."
Corey

Windmill

Part of B-boy floorwork, the windmill is a rotating movement that can be done in either direction, switching the weight from the hands on to the back. The dancer first needs to have perfected the baby freeze.

Starting out

1

Starting off in the baby freeze position, with the weight on the bent arms and toes, the B-boy transfers the weight fully on to his hands. Once safely in the freeze, the head comes down on to the ground and he can begin the rotation movement.

Lifting up

2

Keeping his head down and his hips up, the B-boy rotates his right leg through the gap between the floor and his body, allowing the left leg to swing upward.

Most of the weight is on the hands

▼ **Freestyle routine**
Breakin' moves can be linked into a seamless routine that includes freezes, headspins, inverts, and L-kicks.

Strength and agility

Street dancers need to be in incredibly good shape and pretty strong to make their moves look effortless. For a B-boy or B-girl, floorwork requires stamina, discipline, and agility, and developing these skills demands practice on a regular basis. They need to stay in shape, and it's important to warm up well and stretch out muscles to keep them supple and prevent injury. Eventually, some B-boys and B-girls create their own routines but it's important to master the basics first.

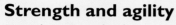

On the back

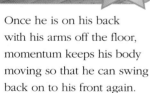

3

Once he is on his back with his arms off the floor, momentum keeps his body moving so that he can swing back on to his front again.

Rotating

4

Keeping his legs out and his head on the floor, the B-boy "cuts" his arms through the shortest distance to gain momentum. He keeps rotating, moving through steps 1 to 3 over and over. The speed at which the move is performed gives the impression of a perfect, continuous "windmill" motion of the legs.

In a freestyle breakin' routine, anything goes

Tutting

DO try this at home!

Tutting was originally inspired by Egyptian hieroglyphics—the name is an abbreviation for the Egyptian pharaoh Tutankhamun. A form of popping, tutting is all about creating right angles using the arms and hands (sometimes the body and fingers). In the 10 poses below, the hands are neat with the fingers together and thumb tucked in.

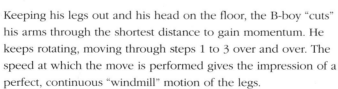

Old style vs. new style

Old style

The original dances that came out of the nightclubs or from the streets during the 1970s and 80s are referred to as "old style"—they include locking, popping, B-boying, waacking, and vogueing. These were the original forms of the dances, with their own styles and rules. Old-style hip-hop is associated with nylon tracksuits and high-top sneakers, as worn by the Rock Steady Crew in the 1980s.

Rock Steady Crew

New style

Although many of the original "street" techniques are still part of new style, there are no rules that have to be followed. New style is an evolution of old style and is more flexible and open. Justin Timberlake uses a new-style approach in many of his music videos.

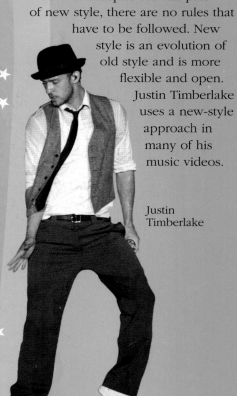

Justin Timberlake

Street styles

The label "street dance" describes a whole variety of dance styles that have evolved since the 1970s. **These dances began on the streets**—in open spaces and street corners—as well as at block parties and nightclubs. When they were created, they couldn't be learned in a class or dance studio—they are social dances that developed in response to the music that was popular at the time.

House dance

In nightclubs such as Warehouse in Chicago and The Loft in New York City, house music began to take over from disco in the 1980s. As clubbers responded to the new faster beats, house dance developed, which is defined by fast, complicated footwork and "jacking"—a pulsing movement of the chest. It is also influenced by elements of Lindy Hop, and Latin and African moves.

Waacking dance moves

Waacking and vogueing

These two related dance styles were both created in nightclubs in the 1970s but on opposite sides of the US. On the East Coast, the style known as waacking was danced to disco music, and on the West Coast, vogueing was danced to house music and was inspired by the model poses that appeared in the fashion magazine *Vogue*. In both styles, the focus is on the arms, which are fast and expressive, creating shapes and poses, often above the head. Madonna's video for her hit "Vogue" in 1990 made vogueing an international dance craze.

Clown dancers from the documentary *Rize* perform with Tommy the Clown

Clowning and krumping

Tommy the Clown created the dance style "clowning" after his style of dance entertainment at children's birthday parties evolved into a popular dance movement that spilled out on to the streets. During dance "battles," the style evolved into "krumping," which is a more raw and passionate form of clowning. Krumping has been featured in several feature movies and documentaries, including the fascinating *Rize* (see page 123).

Li'l C krumping in the 2004 David LaChapelle documentary *Rize*

Freestyle

Freestyle is all about moving to the music freely and individually. It's about a dancer's personal interpretation of the music—a form of improvisation and self-expression. A freestyle dance cannot be planned or choreographed, it has to be "of the moment." In freestyle street dance competitions, the most important skill is "musicality"—matching movements to the beat and melodies of the track so that the body and music become one.

Freestyle street dance in Paris

Crews *and companies*

Street dance and hip-hop started in the 1970s in the US and soon spread **to create a global dance community**. Now there are successful dance crews and companies in cities all around the world. What is the difference between a crew and a company? Crews tend to take part in "battles" and competitions while companies perform their amazing acts in theaters, or in movies and on television. Although companies don't usually "battle," there are some exceptions.

The Electric Boogaloos

Jabbawockeez

Super Cr3w

US

Street dance began in the US in the early 1970s. Pioneers of the locking style (see page 126) were The Lockers and The Electric Boogaloos, with The Rock Steady Crew, among others, developing B-boying and hip-hop (see page 127). Rennie Harris Puremovement company brought hip-hop dance to the theater with award-winning shows such as *Rome and Jewels*, based on Shakespeare's *Romeo and Juliet*. Crews like Jabbawockeez, Super Cr3w, and Quest Crew became famous after winning the prime-time TV show *America's Best Dance Crew*. Competition is always fierce at street-dance contests such as Battle of the Year, which has been won by US crews (Style Elements and Rock Force)—while Methods of Havik and Endangered Species have won the UK B-Boy Championships.

UK

Hip-hop dance was first seen in the UK during the late 1970s and is now showcased by many talented UK crews and companies. The British crew Plague has twice won the US's World Hip-hop Championships. Breakin' Convention, an international festival of hip-hop dance theater in London, has thrown the spotlight on many UK crews and companies. Hip-hop company Boy Blue Entertainment won a prestigious Olivier Award for its theater production *Pied Piper* in 2007, and ZooNation Dance Company staged the award-winning show *Into the Hoods* in 2008. Television talent show *Britain's Got Talent* made stars out of street dancer George Sampson and crews Diversity and Flawless.

ZooNation

Europe

Across Europe, street dance crews and companies are achieving international fame. In Sweden, Bounce Street Dance Company has toured around the world with shows including *Bounce* and *Insane in the Brain*. In France, Compagnie Käfig and Franck II Louise have created hip-hop dance shows for the theater. French crews Wanted, Vagabonds, and Pockemon crews have won either or both the Battle of the Year and the UK B-Boy Championships. The German crew Flying Steps has won Battle of the Year several times and has a worldwide following.

Flawless

Vagabonds (France)

Flying Steps (Germany)

Russia

There is a small but passionate following for B-boying in Russia. The crew Top 9, established in 2001 in St. Petersburg, is the only Russian crew to have won either the UK B-Boy Championships or the Battle of the Year—they won both in 2008.

South Korea

B-boying became very popular in South Korea during the 1980s, mainly through exposure to US movies and music videos. Soon Korean crews were competing in B-boying events, and arriving with a bang. Korean crews—Jinjo Crew, Expression, Gamblerz, Last for One, and Extreme—have won Battle of the Year six times in the last 10 years. Four Korean crews—Project Corea, Project Soul, Drifterz, and T.I.P.—have also won the UK B-Boy Championships.

Top 9

Jinjo Crew

Gamblerz

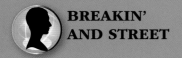

Michael **Jackson**

❝ *Dancers come and go in the twinkling of an eye but the dance lives on.* **❞**

Biography

1958: Born in Gary, Indiana, the seventh of nine children.

1965: Michael and Marlon joined their brothers—Jackie, Tito, and Jermaine—in their band, The Jackson 5.

The Jackson 5 performing in the 1970s

1971: Jackson began his solo career with the hit single "Got To Be There."

1982: *Thriller* was released—the biggest-selling album of all time—followed by several spectacular music videos.

1984: A star was dedicated to Jackson on Hollywood Boulevard's Walk of Fame.

1988: A sell-out tour for the album *Bad* visited 15 countries.

1995: Danced with his sister Janet in the music video for "Scream."

2009: Jackson died at his home in Los Angeles. He was 51.

2010: Inducted into the Dance Hall of Fame.

Influences

From funk to musicals

Michael said he was influenced by funk singer and dancer James Brown, as well as accomplished dancers Fred Astaire and Gene Kelly. He also loved classic musicals such as *West Side Story*.

Michael Jackson—the King of Pop—was the first artist to create music videos that were actually short movies, with a story as well as **thrilling dance performances**. Throughout his career, his videos and his stage shows were extraordinary productions. He was a dancer with a natural gift, and even invented several unique moves.

Michael Jackson performs the "moonwalk"

Moonwalk

Michael Jackson first revealed the famous "moonwalk" when he performed "Billie Jean" at the Motown 25: Yesterday, Today, Forever celebration in 1983. The move uses the technique of gliding from the funk style popping (see page 126). It gives the illusion of walking forward while actually moving backward.

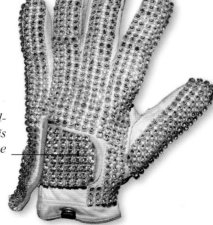

Jackson wore this crystal-studded glove during his "moonwalk" performance

A scene from the "Beat it" music video

Beat it

The video to "Beat it" was one of the first music videos to feature a large cast of dancers performing an intricately synchronized routine. The storyline may have been influenced by *West Side Story* (see page 106), which was one of Jackson's favorite movies, and the final scenes feature two gangs having a "dance off" or "battle." The choreographer Michael Peters also dances in the video, which was released in 1983.

Scene from the music video for *Thriller*

Thriller

A boyfriend is walking his girlfriend home when he turns into a ghoul with a band of zombie followers—this is the story in the 14-minute music video for "Thriller" and it had an amazing impact on audiences worldwide when it was released in December 1983. The length and grand scale of the video were very unusual for the time, and so were the story and stylized choreography. Jackson's moves are incredibly precise, and the "zombies" perform gliding and popping dance steps, too. The infectious quality of the "Thriller Dance" means that it has been re-created by dancers around the world.

King of Pop

Wearing 1930s outfits in a scene from *Smooth Criminal*

Smooth Criminal

The staging and choreography for "Smooth Criminal" are set in the 1930s and are hugely influenced by classic musicals such as *Guys and Dolls*. The dance routine in the music video released in 1988 included some brand-new dance moves, which reappeared in many of Jackson's live performances, including his Bad (1988-9), Dangerous (1992-3), and HIStory (1996-7) world tours. One move—a gravity-defying lean—relied on a specially designed shoe.

Pop performers

Many singers can dance, but only the best dancers are able to create something new and exciting on stage. The singer–dancers featured on these pages all **blend different dance styles** in a dynamic way, and have even developed new moves to express their music. They stage spectacular live shows and create exciting music videos with thrilling dance routines for their songs.

◀ **MC Hammer** popularized the dance move known as "The Running Man." He was a rapper and entertainer who reached his peak in the early 1990s with the release of the hit single "U Can't Touch This." Greatly influenced by James Brown, MC Hammer was known as much for his dance skills as for his music. His shows were spectacular with a large crew of backing dancers.

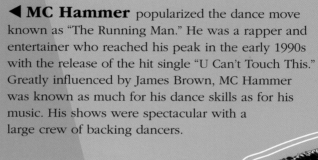

▶ **Janet Jackson** has been responsible for creating some of the most iconic dance videos of all time—including "Nasty" (1986), "Rhythm Nation" (1989), and "Rock with U" (2008). Her live shows are always dazzling, with groundbreaking concepts such as her Velvet Rope tour in 1998, which was influenced by Broadway musicals. There was plenty of complicated choreography and spectacular costumes to showcase Jackson's singing and dancing.

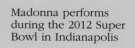

◀ **Will Smith** began his music career as a character called "The Fresh Prince," acting as MC in a hip-hop outfit with DJ Jazzy Jeff and Clarence Holmes (Ready Rock C). The dancing he performs in his music videos, such as "Gettin' Jiggy With It" (1998) and "Switch" (2005), have been copied in clubs around the world.

Madonna performs during the 2012 Super Bowl in Indianapolis

▶ **Usher** sang and danced in a band called NuBeginning when he was 11 years old. In 1991, he competed on the TV show *Star Search* and won a record deal. Usher's amazing dance skills are clear to see in his music video for "Pop ya Collar" (2001), where he plays four characters: a factory worker spinning on a conveyor belt; a businessman doing dance moves on the roof of a car; a football player doing a victory somersault; and a clubber getting down on the dance floor.

▼ **Justin Timberlake** was part of the Mickey Mouse Club on television in the early 1990s, then joined boy band 'N Sync in 1995 before becoming a solo artist. He danced his way through music videos and live performances with flair and ease. For his first album *Justified* in 2002, and his debut single "Like I Love You," he performed Marty Kudelka's laid-back LA new-style choreography, which became hugely influential around the world.

◀ **Madonna** studied dance at the University of Michigan, then moved to New York City to work as a backup dancer. After she became a singer, dance always played a huge part in her music videos and live performances. By showcasing them in her videos, Madonna made dance styles such as vogueing (from her single "Vogue" in 1990) and krumping (from "Hung Up" in 2005) globally popular. Madonna's tours, including Blond Ambition, and her appearances at major events such as the MTV Music Awards and the Super Bowl, always feature cutting-edge dance trends.

◀ **Jennifer Lopez** took dance lessons from a young age. She started her career on Broadway and in rap-music videos and worked as a backup dancer for Janet Jackson. She also starred as a "Fly Girl" dancer on the TV series *In Living Color*. J. Lo, as she became known, began her singing career in 1999 and it was only natural that her music videos and live performances would be driven by dance.

▲ **Justin Bieber** was signed by Usher in 2008. A year later, his debut album *My World*, sold more than a million copies in the US, UK, and Canada. The video for "Somebody to Love" included some of the best street dancers in the world, including the Poreotics Crew, The Beat Freaks, The Syrenz, Medea Sirkas, and B-boy Fly.

137

Glossary

avante-garde This term is used to refer to works of art (including dance) that are pioneering or experimental.

ballerina A title given to a very high-ranking female dancer in a ballet company.

battles Dance competitions between street dancers, either solo or in crews.

B-boys/B-girls Hip-hop dancers who went wild during the instrumental "break" in a track. They were called "breakers" or "break girls" or "break boys"—now shortened to "B-girls" and "B-boys."

Broadway The street of theaters in New York City, where all the top-quality shows are staged.

character role In ballet, a part that doesn't involve ballet technique. The dancer or actor doesn't wear special shoes, and moves around the stage normally, often without dancing.

choreography The arrangements of positions, steps, and movements that make up a single dance, or a whole performance. People who create choreography are called choreographers.

composer Someone who puts notes together to create a piece of music.

corps de ballet The members of a ballet company (usually junior dancers) who perform as a group, doing precise steps in unison.

crew A group or team of street dancers. They might "battle" with other crews in competitions.

danseur A male ballet dancer. A principal male is called a *premiere danseur*, or *danseur noble*.

folk A style of traditional dance, music, or costume that has been developed over time by a particular group of people, rather than being invented by one person.

freestyle To dance freely and interpret the music rather than follow a set pattern of steps or movement.

formation Group ballroom dancing in which all the couples do the same basic dance, but they move in different directions to make a series of lines and patterns on the floor.

Hip-hop Music that developed in the 1970s. It has a strong beat and sometimes includes rapping. Hip-hop dancing is dancing to this style of music.

impresario Someone who puts on, and often finances, entertainments of all kinds.

improvise To make up as you go along, instead of following set steps and movements. Some modern dance choreographers include improvised sections in their work.

leading role In a ballet, contemporary dance work, or musical, a central or starring part. There are usually two leading roles, one for a man and one for a woman.

libretto The story a ballet tells. In musicals and opera, the term *libretto* describes all the words involved in the production. Someone who writes a *libretto* is called a *librettist*.

MC Short for master of ceremonies (or microphone controller). In hip-hop, it's someone who raps over the music.

pas de deux A dance for two people. In classical ballet, a *pas de deux* starts with a slow section for the male and female dancer, called the *adagio*. After this, there are four solos, or variations (male, female, male, female), then at the end, the dancers do a fast part together—this is called the *coda*.

pointe Dancing on tiptoe in ballet, using special blocked shoes for support and protection. Also called *en pointe*.

posture The way people, including dancers, hold and carry their bodies.

production The specific arrangement, set design, and costume design of a ballet or musical.

promenade In ballroom dancing, a position in which the partners are in hold and looking the same way instead of facing each other.

prop (short for property) An object, such as a hat, an umbrella, or even a piece of furniture, used as part of a theatrical or dance performance.

repertoire The collection of works that a dance or theater company is able to perform at any one time—because the artists have learned it, and the necessary costumes and sets are available.

revival A new production of an old ballet or musical, often many years after it first appeared.

ritual An action that has a religious or solemn purpose. Ritual dances have always been important in certain cultures.

routine In stage and movie dance, a choreographed sequence of steps, either for a performance or in class. In a ballet class, the terms "combination" or "*enchaînment*" are more common.

score The music for a ballet, contemporary dance, or musical, written out for all the instruments in an orchestra.

sequence A form of group ballroom dancing in which all the couples perform the same steps, in the same direction, at the same time, often moving in a big circle around the room.

social dancing Any dancing that is done purely for enjoyment rather than for ritual purposes, or as a performance.

solo A dance performed by one person only.

stage set The furnishings, props, and scenery that create the surroundings for a performance. For dance performances, the stage has to be clear, so sets usually take up only the back and sides of the stage.

suite A collection of short musical pieces taken from a longer work. One of the most famous is the Nutcracker Suite, which comes from Tchaikovsky's ballet *The Nutcracker*.

synchronized Happening at exactly the same time. Groups of dancers can perform synchronized movements to great effect.

syncopation In music and dancing, syncopation is stressing beats that would normally be unstressed. These are called "off-beats."

travesty role A part that is played by a man dressed as a woman, or a woman dressed as a man. The Ugly Sisters in *Cinderella* are travesty roles.

West End A central area in London, UK, with many theaters, where all the top-quality shows are staged.

Index

Acknowledgments

Dorling Kindersley would like to thank: Caroline Hunt for proofreading and Helen Peters for the index. Anjana Nair and Neha Sharma for design assistance, and Roma Malik for editorial assistance. For help and advice with the photo shoot: Abi Owens at ZooNation Dance Company, Carrie-Anne Ingrouille, Emma Ponsford at Breakin' Convention, Honey Kalaria at Honey's Dance Academy, Corinne Delaney (www.delaneyacademy.com), Karolina Szmit, Victoria Foster, and Manisha Majithia; and the dancers: Isadora Durkin, Natalie Bartlett, Liam North, Natasha Patel, Nikita Odedra, Shrina Amit Saujani, and Corey Culverwell. **The author would like to thank**: Ian Chilvers, Gemma Fletcher, Stuart Jenner, Lyndon Wainwright, and Stephen Xue.

The publisher would like to thank the following for their kind permission to reproduce their photographs:

(Key: a-above; b-below/bottom; c-centre; f-far; l-left; r-right; t-top)

5 Dreamstime.com: Sabri Deniz Kizil (bc); Lemony (bl); Mykira (bl/purple); Anna Velichkovsky (br/blue); Natalia Kuchumova (br). 6 Corbis: Li An / Xinhua Press (cla); Rikard Stadler / Demotix (clb, clb/dance). Dreamstime.com: Sabri Deniz Kizil (c); Anna Velichkovsky (clb/labels); Natalia Kuchumova (tl). Robbie Jack Photography: (bl). 7 Dreamstime.com: Sabri Deniz Kizil (cla/labels); Mykira (tl); Lemony (clb/Labels). Paul B. Goode: (cla). Stage Entertainment: Manuel Harlan (clb). Paul Hampartsoumian: (bl). 8-9 Corbis: Li An / Xinhua Press. 10 Alamy Images: Interfoto (tl); Mary Evans Picture Library (bc). The Bridgeman Art Library: Catlin, George (1794-1872) / Bibliotheque Nationale, Paris, France / Giraudon (br); Gerome, Jean Leon (1824-1904) / Private Collection (tr). 11 Alamy Images: PhotoStock-Israel (br); Lebrecht Music and Arts Photo Library (tr). Corbis: Dave Hunt / epa (tc). Dreamstime.com: F9photos (cl). 13 Robbie Jack Photography: (c). 14 akg-images: Sotheby's (c). Reuters: Alexander Natruskin (br). 15 akg-images: (tl). Alamy Images: Hemis (r). Reuters: Laszlo Balogh (clb). 16 Alamy Images: Israel images (clb); Interfoto (tr). 16-17 Alamy Images: imagebroker. 17 akg-images: (cr). Alamy Images: Ingolf Pompe 70 (tl). 18 akg-images: RIA Nowosti (t). Alamy Images: Terry Harris (bl). 18-19 Alamy Images: Lebrecht Music and Arts Photo Library (c). 19 Getty Images: Xavier Florensa (tr). 20 Corbis: Burstein Collection (cl); Hulton-Deutsch Collection (bl); Leszek Szymanski / Epa (cb). 20-21 Corbis: Hugh Sitton. 21 Corbis: Jorge Silva / Reuters (tc). Getty Images: Gianni Ferrari (cra). 22 Press Association Images: Fernando Vergara / AP (cl). TopFoto.co.uk: Rose Deakin / Chilepic (br). 22-23 Corbis: Stuart Westmorland. 23 Corbis: Lindsay Hebberd (tc). Dreamstime.com: Tokarsky (r). 24 Alamy Images: Howard Sayer (l). Rossah Bendahman: (crb). Dorling Kindersley: Powell-Cotton Museum, Kent (tc). 24-25 Getty Images: Adrian Dennis. 25 akg-images: africanpictures (br). Reuters: Will Burgess (tr). 26 Getty Images: India Today Group (t). 26-27 Alamy Images: John Warburton-Lee Photography (c); Patrick Ward (t). Corbis: Tim Mosenfelder (b). 27 Alamy Images: Alison Thompson (tc). 28 Alamy Images: Imagery India (clb); Rohan J (clb/Idakka); Jane Williams (tc). Corbis: Andrew Mills / Star Ledger (cl). Getty Images: AFP (bl, bc); PhotosIndia.com (cla). 28-29 Corbis: Photosindia. 29 akg-images: Bildarchiv Steffens (tr). 30 Corbis: Jamal Nasrallah (c). Getty Images: Guang Niu (tr); Yagi Studio (tl). 30-31 Corbis: So Hing-Keung. 31 Getty Images: Bruno Vincent (tr). Lebrecht Music and Arts: Haga Library (tl). 32-33 Corbis: Rikard Stadler / Demotix. 32 Corbis: Rikard Stadler / Demotix (r). 34 Alamy Images: The Art Archive (bc). Dreamstime.com: Pilarts (t). Getty Images: Apic (c). TopFoto.co.uk: (cr). 35 akg-images: Peter Weiss (cla). Alamy Images: Interfoto (tl). Getty Images: Disney ABC Television Group (br); Ferdinand van Reznicek (cr). Mary Evans Picture Library: Rank / Ronald Grant Archive (bl). 36 Alamy Images: Geoff A Howard (l); Patrick Ward (br). 37 Corbis: Zeng Yi / Xinhua Press (cl). Getty Images: Ralf Juergens (tl). 38 akg-images: (bl). Getty Images: De Agostini (tl, tr). 38-39 Vita M Photos. 39 akg-images: RIA Nowosti (bc). Alamy Images: tarczas (tr). 40 Alamy Images: Peter Horree (cl). Corbis: Lebrecht Music & Arts (cb). 41 Dreamstime.com: Derektenhue (bl). Getty Images: Win Initiative (r). 42 The Bridgeman Art Library: Peter Newark American Pictures (tr). Corbis: Luong Thai Linh / epa. 42-43 Alamy Images: Henry Westheim Photography. 43 Alamy Images: Photos 12 (bc); Pictorial Press Ltd (tr). 45 Getty Images: Jennifer Boggs (tc). 46 Reuters: Chaiwat Subprasom (l). 46-47 TopFoto.co.uk: Mark Ellidge / ArenaPAL. 47 Alamy Images: mark downey (tr). Corbis: Catherine Karnow (crb). Dreamstime.com: Anky10 (bl). 48 Corbis: Antonio Lacerda (bl). Reuters: Chaiwat Subprasom (r). 49 Alamy Images: Victor Watts (l). Corbis: Hulton-Deutsch Collection (tr); Julie Lemberger (b). 50 Alamy Images: Tom Craig (br). Corbis: Erik Ward / Retna Ltd. (cl). 50-51 Linedance Stompers Germany: (b). 51 Ceroc Enterprises LTD: (tl, tr). 52-53 Robbie Jack Photography. 54 Alamy Images: RIA Novosti (bl). Getty Images: DEA / A. Dagli Orti (ca). Lebrecht Music and Arts: (c, crb). 55 Corbis: Wolfgang Kaehler (clb). Getty Images: Apic (ca); Baron (br). Lebrecht Music and Arts: RIA Novosti (tl). 56 akg-images: (tc). Alamy Images: Lebrecht Music and Arts Photo Library (c). Robbie Jack Photography: (br). 56-57 Alamy Images: Lordprice Collection. 57 Robbie Jack Photography: (cr). 58 Robbie Jack Photography: (cl, bl, cb). 58-59 Robbie Jack Photography. 59 Corbis: Mohamed Omar / Epa (tr). Robbie Jack Photography: (cl, bl, br). 60 Alamy Images: chris stock photography (tc). Corbis: Bojan Brecelj (tl). Getty Images: Rischgitz (clb). 60-61 Robbie Jack Photography. 61 Bill Cooper: (br). Corbis: Leo Mason (crb). Robbie Jack Photography: (tl, tc, tr). 63 Corbis: Robert Wallis (crb). 64 The Bridgeman Art Library: English Photographer, (20th century) / Private Collection (ca). Robbie Jack Photography: (b, tr). 65 Alamy Images: Patrick Baldwin (tl). Robbie Jack Photography: (clb, br). TopFoto.co.uk: Kingwill Marilyn / ArenaPAL (tc); Roger-Viollet (cr). 66 Corbis: BBC (cr). Getty Images: Sven Creutzmann / Mambo Photo (bl); Time & Life Pictures (br). Robbie Jack Photography: (tl). 66-67 Robbie Jack Photography. 67 Getty Images: AFP (tr). Robbie Jack Photography: (tl, crb). 68 Corbis: Bettmann (tc, c). Getty Images: Sasha (bc). 69 Paul Kolnik: (bl, t). TopFoto.co.uk: Boosey and Hawkes / ArenaPAL (br). 70 Corbis: The Art Archive (cla). TopFoto.co.uk: Nigel Norrington / ArenaPAL (bc). 71 Dorling Kindersley: Freed of London (br). Robbie Jack Photography: (tr). 72 Alamy Images: AF archive (bc); RIA Novosti (cl). Corbis: Bettmann (cr). Getty Images: Time & Life Pictures (bl). 72-73 Getty Images: Baron. 73 Alamy Images: RIA Novosti (tl). Corbis: Hulton-Deutsch Collection (c). Rex Features: Reg Wilson (br). TopFoto.co.uk: Lara Platman / ArenaPAL (tr). 74 Getty Images: Time & Life Pictures (tr). 74-75 Robbie Jack Photography. 75 Corbis: Douglas Kirkland (br). Robbie Jack Photography: (tl, tr). 76 Lebrecht Music and Arts: (cla). TopFoto.co.uk: Colin Jones (bl). 76-77 TopFoto.co.uk: Nigel Norrington / ArenaPAL. 77 Corbis: Rune Hellestad (br). Robbie Jack Photography: (tc, cr). 78 Corbis: Bettmann (tc). Lebrecht Music and Arts: (c). Rex Features: Will Stewart (cla). 78-79 Rex Features: Sipa Press. 79 Getty Images: Keystone (tl); Terry O'Neill (crb). Robbie Jack Photography: (bl). 80 Alamy Images: Itar-Tass Photo Agency (bc). Corbis: Bettmann (cla); Hulton-Deutsch Collection (cr). Getty Images: Time & Life Pictures (clb). 81 Corbis: Imaginechina (tr); Jacques Loew / Kipa (tl). Robbie Jack Photography: (b, cr). 82 Corbis: Hulton-Deutsch Collection (cla); Walter McBride (br). Getty Images: AFP (clb). 82-83 Robbie Jack Photography. 83 Corbis: Stephanie Berger (bl). Robbie Jack Photography: (tr, crb). 84-85 Paul B. Goode. 86 Alamy Images: Lordprice Collection (tr); DIZ Muenchen GmbH, Sueddeutsche Zeitung Photo (cl); Interfoto (br). Corbis: Bettmann (bl). 87 Corbis: Bettmann (tc, crb); E.O. Hoppé (bl). 88 Ernestine Ruben (tc) 88 Robbie Jack Photography: (cl). Klaus Lucka (bl). 88-89 Briana Blasko. 89 Yi-Chun Wu / 吳依純 (tr). David Massio Studio: (tl). Shen Wei/ Bruce R. Feeley: (tc). 90 Lebrecht Music and Arts: Arthur Kales / New York Public Library (c). TopFoto.co.uk: ArenaPAL (tc). 90-91 Alamy Images: Arvind Garg. 91 Corbis: Julie Lemberger (tl). Rex Features: Sipa Press (cr). 92 Getty Images: Dario Cantatore (c). Photoshot: Mudrats Alexandra (tr). Reuters: Mike Segar (bl); John Vizcaino (br). 93 Corbis: Angel Medina G. / epa (tr). Getty Images: Quim Llenas (br). Photoshot: Joerg Carstensen (l). 94 Corbis: Bettmann (cl). 94-95 Robbie Jack Photography. 95 Corbis: Leo Mason (tr). Rex Features: Alastair Muir (crb). TopFoto.co.uk: Henrietta Butler / ArenaPAL (tc); Linda Rich / ArenaPAL (cl). 96 Alamy Images: United Archives GmbH (c); Jerome Yeats (tc); Jane Hobson (crb); Zuma Wire Service (br). Corbis: Michal Fludra / Demotix / Demotix (cla). 97 Alamy Images: AlamyCelebrity (tr); Nathan King (tl). 98-99 Stage Entertainment: Manuel Harlan. 100-101 Dreamstime.com: Aurelko; Raja Rc (Curtain). 100 Alamy Images: AF archive (br); Vintage Images (cl). Dreamstime.com: Stephanie Swartz (tr). Getty Images: Buyenlarge (cr). 101 Alamy Images: Mim Friday (cl). Corbis: Brittany Somerset (cr); Roland Weihrauch / dpa (b). 102 Corbis: Hulton-Deutsch Collection (bl). Getty Images: Hulton Archive (c); Evening Standard (tc). 102-103 The Kobal Collection: Warner Bros (b). 103 Corbis: John Springer Collection (br). Rex Features: Everett Collection (cra). 104 Alamy Images: Moviestore collection Ltd (cra). Corbis: Bettmann (cl); John Springer Collection (bc). 105 Alamy Images: AF archive (br). Corbis: Michael Walls (c). Dein Perry's Tap Dogs / Brinkhoff / Mögenburg: (crb). 106 Alamy Images: Photos 12 (bc); AF archive (cb). Lebrecht Music and Arts: Photofest (ca). 106-107 Rex Features: Snap. 107 Getty Images: Greg Wood (br). The Kobal Collection: 20th Century Fox / Chenault (tl). Rex Features: ITV (cra). 108 Alamy Images: Photos 12 (bl); Moviestore collection Ltd (bc, tc, br). Corbis: John Springer Collection (cla). 109 Getty Images: MGM Studios (l). Stage Entertainment: Dewynters (c), Manuel Harlan (br). 110 Alamy Images: Interfoto (br). Getty Images: Redferns (tc). The Kobal Collection: MGM (c). 111 Alamy Images: Photos 12 (tl). Rex Features: David Fisher (b). 112 The Kobal Collection: India Talkies / Madras Talkies (bc). Ashim Samanta / Shakti Films: (cl). 112-113 Rex Features: Eros International / Everett. 113 Corbis: Leo Mason (bc). The Kobal Collection: Dharma Productions (tr). Photoshot: Starstock (c). Rex Features: Everett Collection (crb). 116 Alamy Images: AF archive (c, b). 116-117 Getty Images: Paramount Pictures. 117 Alamy Images: AF archive (bl); Moviestore collection Ltd (tr, cr). Robbie Jack Photography: (cb). 118 Alamy Images: AF archive (tr); Carolyn Jenkins (bl). 118-119 Alamy Images: AF archive (b). Dreamstime.com: Alfonsodetomas (c). 119 Alamy Images: Photos 12 (cr); AF archive (tl). Robbie Jack Photography: (br). 120-121 Paul Hampartsoumian. 122 Alamy Images: AlamyCelebrity (cr). Corbis: Michael Ochs Archives (cl, clb, bc); Jan Butchofsky (crb). Dreamstime.com. 123 Hugo Glendining: Rowen Hawkins (c). Cast of Into The Hoods/Novello Theatre (bl The Kobal Collection: Wild Style (tl). Benson Lee / Elephant Eye Films: (clb). LXD Ventures, LLC: (br). 124 Corbis: James Andanson / Sygma (br); Sayre Berman (cr); Michael Norcia / Sygma (tr). 125 Corbis: Douglas Kirkland (t). Dreamstime.com: Hubis. 126 Corbis: Roger Ressmeyer (cr). Paul Hampartsoumian: (tl). Robbie Jack Photography: (bc). 127 Adidas: (crb). Corbis: David Atlas / Retna Ltd. (tl). Dreamstime.com: Moori (clb). 130 Alamy Images: Pictorial Press Ltd (cl). Getty Images: Dave Hogan (bl). 131 Corbis: Jeff Minton (tr). Getty Images: Matthew Simmons (tl). Benson Lee / Elephant Eye Films: (b). 132 Getty Images: FilmMagic (cr, bl). Paul Hampartsoumian: (tr). 133 Corbis: A2882 Holger Hollemann / dpa (br). Getty Images: AFP (cr, bc). Hugo Glendining: (tc). Paul Hampartsoumian: (cl). Belinda Lawley: (c). Courtesy of Top 9 Crew: (bl). 134 Alamy Images: zechina (crb). Corbis: Bettmann (tc); Neal Preston (tl); Lynn Goldsmith (c); Chris Walter / Retna Ltd.. Dreamstime.com: Asterixvs (clb). 135 Corbis: Michael Dalder / Reuters (r). The Kobal Collection: Optimus Productions (t); Ultimate Productions / Emerson, Sam (bl). 136 Corbis: Henry Diltz (cl); Rick Friedman / Rick Friedman Photography (bl); David Lefranc / Kipa (cb). 136-137 Getty Images: FilmMagic. 137 Corbis: Steve Azzara (bl); Mark Wallheiser / Reuters (tr); Chris Ryan (cb). Getty Images: FilmMagic (br); KMazur (tl). 138 Alamy Images: Interfoto (bl). 141 Vita M Photos: (br)

Jacket images: Front: Dreamstime.com: Luceluceluce t/ (background); Fotolia: Ellerslie (glitter); Back: Dreamstime.com: Luceluceluce t/ (background); Fotolia: Ellerslie (glitter)

All other images © Dorling Kindersley
For further information see: www.dkimages.com